THE FELLOWSHIP OF CHRISTIAN ATHLETES

THE GREATEST
COACH EVER

THE HEART OF A COACH® SERIES

THE FELLOWSHIP OF CHRISTIAN ATHLETES

THE GREATEST COACH EVER

TONY DUNGY, DAVID ROBINSON, TOM OSBORNE AND OTHERS
—————— PAY TRIBUTE TO THE ——————
TIMELESS WISDOM AND INSIGHTS OF
JOHN WOODEN

Revell

a division of Baker Publishing Group
Grand Rapids, Michigan

This book is dedicated to John Wooden, his family, and to every coach who has continued Coach's legacy of being a teacher first and a coach second.

Contents

THE GREATEST
COACH EVER

INTRODUCTION

"Coach"

On July 29, 2009, *Sporting News Magazine* did the unthinkable. The publication posted the 50 greatest coaches of all time. That's right—of all time! What an incredible challenge to narrow down the list to just 50!

An even greater challenge was choosing who received the number one spot. Who would you pick as the "greatest coach ever"? According to *Sporting News Magazine's* list, John Wooden deserved the top honor.

Why Coach Wooden? Maybe it was because he won 10 national championships at UCLA. Perhaps it was because he became the coach that all the other coaches looked to as the benchmark of success. Either way, John Wooden was crowned the ultimate "Coach," a title that players, friends, fans, admirers and others have called him for more than 75 years.

Actually, Coach never wanted this award, and he felt uncomfortable being tagged with the title. He preferred someone else to be recognized. His reaction may provide some insight as to why he is the greatest. He coached with humility and confidence. He learned the art of mixing together these two seemingly opposite traits—a feat that many others failed to accomplish.

His purpose in coaching was to instill greatness in others. He was committed to teaching, inspiring and motivating people, and he empowered his players to do great things.

For Coach, greatness never had anything to do with himself. He never looked in the mirror when it came to success or accomplishments. Greatness was reflected in focusing on others. He was consumed with the simple principle he called competitive greatness—"not be the best, but be the best that you can be." With that message, tens of thousands of lives have been profoundly touched by this legendary coach.

Coach's impact has swept through every sport in every way possible. Name a topic and Coach has covered it in his teaching. Philosophy of coaching, definition of winning, parenting, persevering through difficult situations, integrity, definition of success, teamwork, reaching noble goals, true friendship, and life mission statements are just a few that will be applied in the following pages.

At the Fellowship of Christian Athletes, we have a tradition that has occurred at every summer camp for more than 50 years. On the last night of camp, we have an open mic session when athletes come forward and share how camp has impacted their lives. It is always the highlight of the entire week of camp.

When I read that John Wooden received the title "Greatest Coach of All Time," I pictured what an open mic session for him might look like. I imagined an endless line of the players, coaches and people who had been directly and indirectly influenced by Coach sharing countless stories of personal impact. What an incredible night of celebration that would have been!

Coach would have been surprised and blessed to hear the life-changing difference that he made through the years, and we would all be challenged and encouraged to leave such a legacy ourselves! Well, this book is that open-mic session. We have chosen 39 men and women from all walks of life to share how Coach marked them on their journey of sports and faith. And, of course, timeless wisdom from Coach Wooden is sprinkled throughout every page. As a loyal and enthusiastic supporter of FCA since its beginning, Coach was thrilled to do this book just for FCA.

We are thankful that Coach Wooden never stopped coaching. Even after he officially retired, he lived out the adage, "once a coach, always a coach." He blessed us beyond measure because he used the game of basketball to coach people about life. As a result, we are all changed.

Enjoy!

Dan Britton
Executive Vice President
Fellowship of Christian Athletes

We invite you to join in Coach Wooden's open-mic session by visiting www.greatestcoachever.com and leaving a tribute to Coach Wooden or another coach who was "the greatest coach ever" in your life.

1

Good Things Take Time

BY LES STECKEL

President, Fellowship of Christian Athletes
and Former NFL Coach

We tend to forget that all good things take time.
JOHN WOODEN

It was the dream of a lifetime. In 1984, I was named head coach of the Minnesota Vikings and at the time was the second youngest head coach in the NFL. My coaching career was barely a decade old and after five seasons as an assistant, I had replaced the retiring Bud Grant.

But in four short months, I went from being a popular assistant to filling the dreaded role of hated head coach. My Marine style of leadership and discipline and my failure to nurture relationships with my coaching staff set the tone for a rough campaign. After the team finished 3-13, my dream quickly turned into a nightmare. I was fired after just one season.

Since that time, I've come to appreciate the wisdom of Coach Wooden's famous words: "Good things take time." Did I deserve more time to prove myself in Minnesota? I don't know. But I've been encouraged by a legendary head coach who did get that chance and who I believe best illustrates Coach Wooden's saying. His name is Tom Landry.

Shortly after I left the Vikings, I spent some time with Coach Landry in his home. As we sat in his living room, he told me an interesting story about his early years coaching the Dallas Cowboys. His team won five or fewer games in each of his first five seasons including a 0-11-1 start as a rookie coach in 1960.

"Les, you weren't as fortunate as I was," he told me. "You won three games your first year. I didn't win any."

Naturally, the Dallas fans were impatient and wanted results. The legendary general manager, Tex Schramm, called the team owner, Clint Murchison, Jr., and told him they needed to make a change: Coach Landry would be fired. Murchison told Schramm that he would call him back after the weekend. Murchison called on the following Monday and surprised his general manager by giving Coach Landry a 10-year contract.

"We have the right man," Murchison said. "Good things are going to happen. But it takes time."

Coach Landry eventually proved Murchison right and led the Dallas Cowboys for 29 seasons. During that time, Dallas won two Super Bowls, five NFC titles, 13 Divisional titles, and compiled a 270-178-6 record.

That scenario likely wouldn't happen in today's day and age. Our society is conditioned to be impatient and expect instant results. We live by two words: performance and pressure. If you can't perform, you're out, and the pressure to succeed is intense.

We need to substitute another word: patience. Very few people exercise patience today. Even Coach Wooden admitted once in an interview that if he had coached today, who knows what would have happened to his career. He didn't launch his first few years at UCLA by winning, and it took him 14 years before he won his first championship there.

Can you imagine what we might have missed out on if coaches like Tom Landry and John Wooden had not been given time to build the foundation for their successful programs?

Many innovations to the games of football and basketball might not have been conceived. And, more importantly, two of the greatest coaches of all time might not have been afforded the sizable platforms that have impacted countless lives.

Coach Wooden modeled this principle of patience in his coaching. When I became a coach, I found myself watching him during games and wanting to emulate him. He was always so calm and poised when he was on the bench. I didn't know he held a cross in his hands during every game until years later. He was fiercely competitive, yet he exuded a gentle spirit. You could tell he had such passion for his players. I wanted to be like that. I wanted to be a Christian example for others.

But the journey to understanding Coach Wooden's principle of patience was difficult at times. I think about when I was the offensive coordinator for the Tennessee Titans. In 1997, when the team moved from Houston to Nashville, our stadium was not yet finished. Our home games during the first season were at the Liberty Bowl in Memphis. The city of Memphis wanted the franchise, but it went to Nashville instead. As a result, the fans there were bitter. They made a point to boo us during games and cheer for the opposing team.

The next season, we played our home games at Vanderbilt University in Nashville where the city said it would fully support us. But at each game, only a fraction of the crowd would cheer for us while 30,000 others rallied for the visiting teams. Three years later, after struggling to gain a faithful fan base, we finally got to play in our own stadium—the Coliseum. That year, we went undefeated at home before losing to St. Louis 23-16 in Super Bowl XXXIV. Good things take time.

Wooden's principle of patience is firmly rooted in God's Word, and I have found encouragement in such Scriptures as Psalm 27:14: "Wait for the Lord; be courageous and let your heart be strong. Wait for the Lord."

In 1984, I was devastated when the Vikings fired me. It wouldn't be the last time I lost a job that I really loved. I've learned it takes patience and courage to get through tough circumstances and trust in God to help you accept the truth found in Romans 8:28: "We know that all things work together for the good of those who love God: those who are called according to His purpose."

I can now look back and see that God has been with me and leading me to this point in my life. I never would have thought I'd be the president of Fellowship of Christian Athletes and helping the ministry ensure it has a long and healthy future.

Coach Wooden's legacy was built over a 100-year period of time. Imagine how his impact might have diminished had he not understood the truth behind his own words: "Good things take time." I'm thankful to have had him as an example that I can continue to follow.

WOODEN'S WISDOM

Before success comes patience. . . . When we add to our accomplishments the element of hard work over a long period of time, we'll place a far greater value on the outcome. When we are patient, we'll have a greater appreciation of our success.

TRAINING TIME

1. Has there ever been a time in your life when someone gave you more than one chance to prove yourself?

2. How have you seen the phrase "good things take time" play out in your own life?

3. Read Romans 8:28. How does this verse give you encouragement to pursue patience in your current situation?

PRAYER

Father, thank You that You work all things together for my good. Help me to exhibit patience and courage in my life as I wait on Your perfect timing.

Les Steckel is the president of Fellowship of Christian Athletes. He previously coached for 23 years in the NFL. Steckel was head coach of the Minnesota Vikings in 1984 and offensive coordinator of the Tennessee Titans during its Super Bowl XXXIV run during the 1999-2000 season.

2

Success Redefined

BY JIM TRESSEL

Head Coach, Football, Ohio State University

Success is peace of mind that is the direct result of self satisfaction in know-ing you did your best to become the best that you are capable of becoming.
JOHN WOODEN

As a boy growing up in Mentor, Ohio, I rooted my heart out for the Cleveland Browns. My father, Lee Tressel, was a very success-ful coach at Baldwin-Wallace College for 33 years. In fact, the Browns maintained practice facilities on campus there.

But early on, I learned that winning is not simply scoring the most points. In fact, true success has little to do with the fi-nal score. Today, as coach of a major college football team, I be-lieve this truth more than ever and try to practice it every day. Let me tell you how I discovered that coaching has to do with much more than *X*s and *O*s, and how John Wooden helped shape the person that I am today.

Sitting in front of our brand-new Zenith color television set, I watched every second of UCLA's NCAA championship basket-ball game in 1964. The Bruins prevailed over Duke 98-83. Although I was just 12, I was fascinated by how easily Coach

Wooden's team dominated both ends of the court despite having a much shorter team. After the game, Wooden told his team, "I am immensely proud of you. You're really the best. You've proved it. Now don't let it change you."

Coach Wooden's response to such an extraordinary victory might seem peculiar in today's win-at-all-costs society. But as far as I'm concerned, that was great coaching!

The first time I had the chance to meet Coach Wooden was in 1983. I was an assistant at Ohio State, and I'd been a fan of his for a long time. He happened to be here in Columbus, Ohio, and Earle Bruce, our head coach, took the whole staff to meet him. When I heard him speak, I became enthralled with him.

Part of what attracted me to Coach Wooden was his thoroughness. He wanted to make sure that he was thorough in working with every part of the player—spiritually, academically and attitudinally. It wasn't just going to be about the *X*s and *O*s of the game. Coach Wooden was going to judge how well he succeeded based upon the type of man his player became.

To me, that was very appealing. I saw my dad do the same thing. I saw him bring the players to our house, and I saw much more than football being taught at practice. Games come and go and the rings and trophies get dusty, but the legacy is really what players learn from their experience.

Of all the profound words that Coach Wooden spoke, I've been most impacted by his definition of success: "Success is peace of mind that is the direct result of self-satisfaction in knowing you did your best to become the best that you are capable of becoming."

When I first went to Youngstown State as the head coach in 1986, I wanted to define what it meant to be successful. As a 1-AA football program, our goal was to be the national champion. We were blessed to accomplish that four times. But we wanted to make sure that we followed our own definition of success, which we crafted after Coach Wooden's definition: "Success is the peace of mind and inner-satisfaction knowing that I did the best that I was capable of doing for the group."

I used that definition through 15 years at Youngstown State and now 10 years here at Ohio State. That principle has also helped me keep the proper perspective at both ends of the spectrum—winning and losing. On one hand, if we won some games but knew we didn't do our best, we didn't feel successful. On the other hand, if we did our best but lost, we still succeeded.

I can think of two losses in particular that gave our team two very different feelings. In 2006, our team went undefeated heading into the Bowl Championship Series (BCS) title game as the #1-ranked team in the nation against #2-ranked Florida. Our star receiver, Ted Ginn, Jr., now with the Miami Dolphins, scored on the opening play with a kickoff return for a touchdown. Unfortunately, he sustained a foot injury celebrating afterwards and never stepped on the field again that night. We lost that game 41-14. As you can imagine, we were very disappointed, but not for the reasons most would suspect. It wasn't about the loss. It was about the lack of overall performance that we had as a team and as a coaching staff. Losing is always worse when you know you didn't play your best.

The opposite was true when we faced Texas in the 2009 Fiesta Bowl. We were playing the #3-ranked Longhorns that some thought should be playing in the BCS title game. We lost a hard-fought game on a Colt McCoy touchdown pass with 26 seconds remaining. Our players and coaches prepared and played extremely hard and well, but we came up short. It was a loss, but it felt totally different.

The lessons learned in both disappointing losses certainly prepared us to understand just what it takes to always be at our best. These valuable lessons contributed to a satisfying 2010 Rose Bowl victory versus Oregon.

When Coach Wooden came up with his definition of success, he must have understood the truths found in Proverbs 18:12, where Solomon teaches that "humility comes before honor" (*NIV*), and Psalm 40:4, where David writes, "Blessed is the man who makes the LORD his trust" (*NIV*). It's not the rankings. It's not what the television commentators say. But blessings come to the man who trusts in the Lord. That's true success. It's that peace of mind knowing that you did the best you could.

After Coach Wooden retired in 1975, he was always willing to share what he believed with thousands of coaches. He was a tremendous role model for thousands of aspiring coaches in multiple sports. There were many of us who felt that we had an intimate relationship with him because we hung on his every word.

From a coaching standpoint, some people might have voted for Coach Wooden as the greatest coach of all time because of his record. Some might have voted for him because of the wisdom he passed on to so many coaches. Both reasons show why he was the clear-cut winner. He was the best.

WOODEN'S WISDOM

Winning seems so important, but it actually is irrelevant. Having attempted to give our all is what matters—and we are the only ones who really know the truth about our own capabilities and performance. Did we do our best at this point in our life? Did we leave all we had to give on the field, in the classroom, at the office or in the trenches? If we did, then we are a success—at that stage in our life.

TRAINING TIME

1. How is Wooden's definition of success different than any other definitions of success that you have heard?

2. How does trusting God and putting Him first make you successful?

3. Read Proverbs 18:12. How does having humility bring honor and success?

PRAYER

Father, help me to change my view of success to match Your definition of success. Help me to learn true humility and trust You in all situations.

Jim Tressel is the head football coach at Ohio State University, where he has led the Buckeyes to six Big Ten titles, three Bowl Championship Series National Championship Games, and a 14-0 season in 2002 that resulted in a national title. Tressel also spent 15 years as the head coach at Youngstown State, where his team captured four Football Championship Series (Division 1-AA) titles.

3

First Things First

BY DAVE PASCH

Broadcaster, ESPN and Arizona Cardinals

Don't let making a living prevent you from making a life.
JOHN WOODEN

As a young broadcaster, interviewing Coach Wooden at the 2006 McDonald's All-American Game was the chance of a lifetime. As a Christian, I didn't just want to hear him speak about basketball; I wanted to garner insight into this man's great faith.

During the interview, we discussed basketball and some of the amazing talent represented in the high school all-star game. But off camera, I took the opportunity to ask Coach Wooden about his faith and how he became a Christian. He graciously shared the story of his wife's influence and how at first he attended church and was baptized to please her and her parents.

Coach Wooden also told me how he maintained the daily discipline of reading the Bible and spending time in prayer—a practice that dated back to his childhood days and one that he faithfully continued throughout his entire coaching career. Even as a college student when he would get up early in the morning to study, he would open each study session with a time of devotion in God's Word.

That interview with Coach Wooden has had a lasting impact on my life. As a student of the game, I was certainly aware of his legendary accomplishments, but I found myself even more inspired by the way he balanced his personal affairs with his demanding professional responsibilities.

I didn't always have a strong desire for God-centered priorities. In fact, I didn't have a strong desire for God, period! I wanted to do my own thing and rule my own life. Growing up, all I wanted to do was work at a major sports network or do play-by-play for an NFL team. As a young person in my twenties, I would have cut any corner or stepped on anybody to accomplish that goal.

Yet just as Coach Wooden's faith was encouraged by his wife, Nell, I also found myself transformed as I followed my wife, Hallie's, lead and the Holy Spirit's calling into a relationship with God. When I became a follower of Christ, He helped me change my priorities. That has meant putting Him first.

I've learned to prioritize God into my job. When I'm doing a game, what I say on the air reflects whether I really believe what I profess to believe. Criticizing unfairly or saying something off-color could impact the way people view me. "Well, he says he's a Christian, but look at what he says on the air."

I also put God first in my preparation. In some ways, broadcasting is like coaching or playing sports. I can have nine great games in a row, but if I make a big mistake in the tenth game, that's what people remember. What's the best way to be prepared? By starting my day in prayer and studying the Bible. In doing those two things, I have more energy, passion and empowerment to prepare for my job as best as I can.

Putting first things first also carries over into my duties as a husband and father. Along with my faith, I have committed to making my family the most important part of my existence. When Coach Wooden said, "Don't let making a living prevent you from making a life," he understood that material things never make up for time spent with family.

Coach Wooden always considered his family first when making an important decision. He didn't make a career move without talking to his wife—even the move to UCLA. Their desire was to stay in the Midwest, but when they had the chance to move out West, they took it. But they took it together. Even when success came and his love for the job grew, he didn't put it above his wife and their children. He never risked neglecting his family in some way to pursue other goals. Here was a man who could have done anything and gone anywhere. He could have named his job and his price tag. But he didn't do it. He valued family more than his career.

For me, it all comes back to putting God first. If my relationship with Him isn't right, then neither is my relationship with my wife. If my relationship with my wife or my children is strained, I can't properly prepare for my job.

Out-of-order priorities can quickly turn life upside down. King David is a powerful but sad example. When he put his relationship with God on the back burner, he opened up his heart to lust and covetousness. David's desire for another man's wife led him down a path to adultery and murder; and when he failed to properly prioritize his family, he suffered greatly when his son Absalom was tragically killed.

On the other hand, Jesus is an example of what it looks like to have priorities in order. He spent quality time in prayer and communion with God, knowing how that would impact His ministry. He put His Father first so that He could be full of the Spirit and empowered to help others. In Mark 1:35 we read that, "Very early in the morning, while it was still dark, He got up, went out, and made His way to a deserted place. And He was praying there."

In today's society, too few men and women have grasped this vitally important concept of priorities. I used to be one of them.

But through the biblical account of Christ and the living example of Coach Wooden, I've learned that having my priorities in the right order is the difference between true fulfillment and empty, short-lived dreams.

WOODEN'S WISDOM

People don't spend enough time with their families. They get caught up in material things, thinking those make up life. The pursuit of material possessions often takes precedence over the things that are more lasting, such as faith, family, and friends. Don't allow the lesser values to raise havoc on your family.

TRAINING TIME

1. In your life right now, are you putting first things first?

2. How does Jesus provide an example of having priorities in order?

3. What are some changes you can make to your priorities to make sure your relationship with Jesus Christ is first?

PRAYER

Father, please forgive me for not always putting first things first and not making my relationship with You my number one priority. Help me to reprioritize my life in a way that is pleasing to You and in turn will be a blessing to my family and friends.

Dave Pasch is the radio play-by-play announcer for the NFL's Arizona Cardinals. He also works as a television broadcaster for the ESPN Networks, covering such events as college football, college basketball, the NBA, and the WNBA.

4

God's Playbook

BY BOBBY BOWDEN
Former Head Coach, Football, Florida State University

Drink deeply from great books; especially the Bible.
JOHN WOODEN

Coach Wooden and I share something in common. I'd like to say it was the same number of national championships, but his far outweigh the two football titles I was blessed to win at Florida State. Really, I don't know how anyone could ever duplicate what he did. It's just impossible. Who can argue with the fact that Coach Wooden just might be the greatest coach ever?

What Coach Wooden and I share is of much greater value than a piece of hardware that sits in a trophy case. We both have lived our lives using foundational principles based on God's Word. Reading Coach Wooden's books over the years has reinforced my thinking. He has shown the world that one can live and teach by those principles and still be a winner. Studying the Bible was a "good habit," as he wrote in *Coach Wooden One-on-One*, which started when his father read to him daily. He continued reading the Bible in college, throughout his marriage, and to his children when they were young.

When I got into coaching, I kept a regular Bible reading routine that I maintain to this day. I used to get up at 4:00 A.M. Now that I'm retired, I get up at 4:30 A.M., because I'm so used to getting up that early. I go downstairs, put coffee on for my wife, and get out my Bible and maybe 10 other books about the Bible. I read the Scriptures, and then I read a little from the other books. I do that for about an hour. Then my wife joins me and we read together. That's how we start every day.

During my time at Florida State, I encouraged my staff to also start the day in the Word. Every morning our coaches would meet, we'd begin with a devotional. We'd read Scripture and end with prayer. Seventeen coaches would sit around a table and take turns leading the devotion. I didn't expect them to believe what I believed, but I wanted to hear what they believed.

This carried over to all of our teams. Every Friday night when I talked to the kids before the games, we'd have a devotional. The next day, we would pray before and after the games. I've always joked that the ACLU would be very disappointed in me. I once told our president, "If they ever say anything about it, I'll go underground, because I'm not going to stop."

People might have wondered why I would bring the Bible into my coaching at a state-run institution. Maybe a better question should be, why not? Who could have been a better CEO of our program than the good Lord? And, when you think about it, there are so many principles from the Bible that speak to the challenges facing coaches and athletes.

One of the Bible's foundational teachings is sacrifice. Excellence cannot be achieved unless coaches and players are willing to sacrifice and suffer. They've got to pay the price. For football players, that means going through two-a-days in the heat of summer and spending months away from home—even on school breaks when other students have vacated the campus. For coaches, that means spending long hours into the night watching film, evaluating talent and devising game plans.

Paul set a great example of sacrifice for us when he walked away from his campaign to persecute Christians and became a lowly evangelist. He gave up a life of privilege in exchange for the same persecution he once enforced. Through Paul's life we can understand our call to sacrifice. Romans 8:36 tells us that, "Because of [God] we are being put to death all day long; we are counted as sheep to be slaughtered."

Coach Wooden went through 14 seasons at UCLA before he hit the top. We all have to sacrifice some when we choose to follow the path Christ has laid out for us.

Just like Wooden, I've drawn my strength from the Bible. It has helped me understand that God is in control. I have had my share of bad days throughout my coaching career. There were times when people wanted me to leave and hang in effigy. But it was my faith and belief in God's Word that got me through those tough times.

So remember to follow Coach Wooden's advice to "drink deeply from great books; especially the Bible." Go ahead, the time is now.

WOODEN'S WISDOM

I have always read the Bible. . . . It was a habit I enjoyed very much.
I don't say that with any degree of pride. It was a habit of love,
not one of requirement or drudgery. It wasn't just something to do,
it was never a chore, and I enjoyed it.

TRAINING TIME

1. Do you start each day in God's Word? If not, think of a time you can set aside daily to spend time reading the Bible and in prayer.

2. Where do you draw your strength in times of adversity?

3. How can God's Word give you strength through a tough situation that you are facing now?

PRAYER

Father, thank You for Your Word. Thank You for providing Your game plan for my life through the Bible. Help me to start each day in Your Word and draw from it the strength I need to face life's tough situations.

Bobby Bowden is the former head football coach at Florida State University and a member of the College Football Hall of Fame. In 34 seasons, he led the Seminoles to a pair of national championships and 12 ACC titles.

5

Active Duty

BY DAVID ROBINSON

Hall of Fame NBA Center, San Antonio Spurs

Initiative is having the courage to make decisions and take action.

JOHN WOODEN

Two years. That's how long the San Antonio Spurs waited for me. Needing to build for their future, they risked the first overall pick of the 1987 NBA Draft on a lanky 7' 1" post player from the Naval Academy. The team knew that I would have to fulfill at least two years of active duty to the Navy—or possibly more.

When the Navy excused me early from my commitment, I discovered a harsh reality: Everybody always wants you to be somebody else. The media and fans instantly compared me to other great centers. They wanted me to be like Patrick Ewing or Akeem Olajuwon. As my career continued, people wanted me to be like Michael Jordan and take my team to a title.

But I knew that I wasn't one of those guys. I had to be brave and take the initiative to be myself. That's all I could do.

Coach Wooden was setting an example of courage long before I was born. When he accepted the job at UCLA, he took the initiative to be himself in Los Angeles—heavily influenced even then by

Hollywood—and not change his personality. Coach Wooden was a sensitive, giving, caring and unassuming man in a city where people are obsessed with glitz and glamour. But his teams did not brag; they played with humility. And he was respected for that.

Former players like Bill Walton and Kareem Abdul-Jabbar will tell you that Coach Wooden was one of the men they respect most in their lives. That's a tremendous gift—to have the poise to be yourself and the initiative to impact your environment, without letting your environment impact you. Instead of being changed, he changed everything else.

As a rookie, I took that lesson with me. I didn't know the city well, and I had yet to form relationships with any players. But if I learned anything in the military, it was that good leaders assess the situation and move quickly to address the problem. That's what active duty is all about. That's what initiative is all about.

So, as a rookie, I decided to take initiative and root out the unprofessionalism I observed. Our players needed to respect one another, and we needed to get rid of activities detrimental to our team's success. When I accepted Christ in 1991, my bent toward initiative went even further. I don't know how many teams started their games with prayer, but we did. Right before stepping on the court, we'd circle up and give thanks to God—win or lose. That added character to our team. It helped us see the bigger picture and get past petty distractions.

At first everyone rebelled against the pre-game ritual. But as God's Word says in Joshua 24:15, "As for me and my house, we will serve the LORD" (*KJV*). I thought, *As long as this is my team, we're going to honor God. It might be Tim Duncan's team in a few years, but right now this is how we're going to do it.*

Over the years, that prayer and a respectful attitude became our signature. Toward the end of my career, people from other teams told me they had laughed at us. They would see us praying and thought we were religious nuts. But after spending a little time in our locker room, I remember one player saying, "I wouldn't want to be in any other locker room."

Initiative isn't just about taking a stand. Sometimes it means recognizing the needs of others and showing them love. Active duty means taking action to address real problems that face real people. That's what happened when I founded The Carver Academy.

As I was traveling all over the country, I saw students focused on the wrong things who didn't understand the value of education and character. I dedicated my life to this problem by building a school in San Antonio where kids could get a high-level education and grow through effective character building and leadership programs.

Through the process, I've learned to walk by faith in much the same way the biblical hero David lived his life. When he was a young man, he took initiative on the battlefield. David was nothing more than a shepherd boy, but when he saw the threat that Israel's army was facing by Goliath and his army, he boldly asked, "Who is this uncircumcised Philistine that he should defy the armies of the living God?" (1 Samuel 17:26).

It's fitting that my name is David because I really do have that same type of personality. The irony is that I'm closer in height to Goliath, but on the inside, David's fearless attitude is an accurate picture of me. I'm too simple to be afraid. I really don't know when something is impossible. When I see people standing around, all I can say is, "What are we afraid of? Let's get running and win!"

But my confidence isn't based on arrogance; it is rooted in the understanding that life and death are not in my hands. I don't spend a lot of time worrying about pass or fail. It's not my job to win the war. It's my job to fight. It's not my job to win the race. It's my job to run. That's what active duty looks like for the believer. It's trusting that the LORD is with us and having the faith that He will walk us through every challenge and every purpose. And that's the kind of initiative that Coach Wooden advocated.

Coach Wooden has been an encouragement to me and provided an example that I hope to emulate. He blazed the trail by taking the initiative to love others and stand up for his faith. If I make it to 70 years old and beyond, I still want to be encouraging the younger generations and helping them understand that they too can stand strong and take action "when action is needed."

WOODEN'S WISDOM

People with initiative will act when action is needed.

TRAINING TIME

1. Read Joshua 24:14-15. How did Joshua display courage and initiative in his situation?

2. Are you living your life in "active duty" by taking action to address real problems that face real people?

3. What is one area of your life where God is prompting you to take the initiative to serve others and show them love?

PRAYER

Father, open my eyes to the needs of others around me, and give me the courage to take the initiative to take action to address those needs. Help me to trust in You through every challenge and purpose for my life.

David Robinson is a retired NBA MVP and 10-time All-Star who played his entire 14-year career with the San Antonio Spurs. He led the Spurs to NBA titles in 1999 and 2003 and was a three-time Olympian, winning two gold medals (1992 and 1996) and one bronze medal (1988). Robinson is the founder and chairman of The Carver Academy in San Antonio, Texas.

6

Constructive Correction

BY TONY DUNGY

Former Head Coach, Indianapolis Colts

Criticism and correction differ, especially when it comes to methods and motives. Criticism puts someone down. Correction means I want to help.

JOHN WOODEN

After 15 years of working as an assistant coach in the NFL, I was ready to make the leap. I'd always wanted to be a head coach, and my opportunity had finally arrived. It was 1996, and the Tampa Bay Buccaneers decided to take a chance on a grown-up kid from Jackson, Michigan.

But many people in the league privately wondered if I could do it. I wasn't the type to yell at people. I wasn't the type to get in someone's face. Some questioned if I had what it took. Could I control the players? Would they respond to me? Could a coach with such a mild-mannered demeanor handle an entire team?

There's no question in my mind why some people had these concerns. It had a lot to do with my method of correction. Amid their curiosity and doubt, I couldn't help but wonder if the silent (and sometimes vocal) critics had ever heard about a man I had grown to admire and pattern my coaching style after.

My first introduction to Coach John Wooden was in 1965. I was nine years old at the time, and I remember listening to UCLA's game against Michigan on the radio with my dad. Walt Hazzard and Gail Goodrich beat Cazzie Russell and our hometown favorites 91-80 in the NCAA championship game.

That was the first I'd heard of UCLA basketball. Over the next few years, I saw the Bruins continue winning and producing star players. Then, when I got a little older and started to get interested in the coaching profession, I realized that Coach Wooden was the leader of this phenomenon. It didn't matter who was playing on those teams; he was the one constant that kept the Bruins successful year after year.

I began studying Coach Wooden's philosophies and learned that correction was about helping people improve as a player and person. I was also guided by some coaches who came from a similar school of thought. During my two years playing defensive back for the Pittsburgh Steelers, Chuck Noll impacted me with his approach to discipline. He always corrected his players with the intention of making them better, not just pointing out their mistakes.

And really, that's the biggest difference between criticism and correction. It's all about motives. Harsh criticism is often driven by insecurity or the need to exert power and authority over others. It usually does more damage than good and can quickly tear down one's confidence. On the other hand, correction is rooted in a desire to see people learn and grow. It's about giving them the best chance to succeed.

Coach Wooden's style of teaching and correction greatly influenced me as an NFL head coach. I learned quickly that when an athlete has a problem in his or her personal life or on the field, how you correct that athlete becomes important.

From a distance, Coach Wooden taught me that the goal of correction is to change a player's mindset and speak to his or her heart. His methods, in many ways, mirrored the teaching style of

Jesus. How did Jesus correct? He told stories. He showed examples. He pointed things out. He didn't just say "this is wrong" and "this is right."

Jesus corrected people by getting them to think. He presented analogies using nature and cultural references. Jesus also shared parables that gave His disciples truths to ponder in relatable presentations. One such example is found in Matthew 21:28-31. It's a story of a man and his two sons:

> He went to the first and said, "My son, go, work in the vineyard today." He answered, "I don't want to!" Yet later he changed his mind and went. Then the man went to the other and said the same thing. "I will, sir," he answered. But he didn't go. Which of the two did his father's will?

Jesus was trying to correct His disciples' thinking about the kingdom of God, and this story hit the mark. They correctly answered that it was the first son who had pleased his father. Jesus didn't criticize His disciples' errant mindset or mock their lack of understanding. Instead, He turned it into a significant time of instruction and correction.

Of course, this mode of correction isn't devoid of discipline. There's still a right and a wrong way to go about your business. It reminds me of a story Coach Wooden once told about Bill Walton, a UCLA player who, back in 1971, didn't want to cut his hair. Walton asked Coach, "What if I don't want to cut my hair?" To that, Coach matter-of-factly replied, "You'll be the longest-haired guy on the intramural team."

There are certain rules and protocols that are non-negotiable. The punishment is already set, and everyone knows it. But then, if a rule is broken and you have to correct, it's best to use that discipline as a teachable moment and a time to ask, "Where are we going to go from here?"

One thing that I'm excited to see is the emergence of a new generation of coaches who have built trusting relationships with their players. They are teachers first and coaches second. But it's taken time for people to buy into this new kind of thinking.

As the Colts began contending in the playoffs but failed to win the big games, my style of coaching and correction became the culprit in some people's minds. But once we won Super Bowl XLI, people experienced a shift in their opinions. "Maybe there is something to that," they now say. Winning does tend to validate your methods. And who better to exemplify winning the right way than Coach Wooden? His philosophy has stood the test of time.

People ask all the time if different coaches would have been successful in other eras. There's no doubt that Coach Wooden could have coached in this era. I have the confidence that if he had been coaching in 2010, he would have won championships. And he would have done so by employing the same principled methods that helped his teams win 10 NCAA titles in 12 years— with a soft-spoken delivery, a strong conviction, a sensitive ear, and a firm but fair approach to correction.

WOODEN'S WISDOM

Be slow to correct and quick to commend. No one likes correction, but we learn from it. If we commend before we correct, the person will accept the correction better. But we must listen before we correct. There is usually another side to every story. If we listen to others, they will be more apt to listen to us.

TRAINING TIME

1. How is Wooden's philosophy of correction different than other coaches you have seen?

2. Read Matthew 21:28-32. How does this passage reflect Jesus' style of correction?

3. How can you incorporate this biblical style of correction into your life?

PRAYER

Father, thank You for loving me and helping me grow through correction. Help me to model Jesus' style of correction to those whom I teach and influence.

Tony Dungy is the former head coach of the Indianapolis Colts. He led Indianapolis to victory at Super Bowl XLI and also played for the Pittsburgh Steelers team that won Super Bowl XIII. Dungy, the author of two *New York Times* bestsellers, currently works as a studio football analyst for NBC.

7

Staying True

BY TAMIKA CATCHINGS
WNBA Forward, Indiana Fever

Loyalty is the foundational quality that gets us through hard times. Will we compromise our integrity when temptation is great? Or will we remain loyal to our beliefs and core values?

JOHN WOODEN

It might sound crazy, but tearing my ACL in January 2001 was a good thing. At the time, however, I wouldn't have agreed. The timing was horrible. My dream was to play in the WNBA, and with just five months until the draft, I knew the injury would cost me my dream.

But God was faithful, and despite the doctor's report that I would sit out an entire season, the Indiana Fever took a chance on me with the third overall pick.

Even while I was still recovering, I was calm and had peace, because I knew that God had a purpose for me to fulfill by playing in the WNBA. He was with me every step of the way.

That entire season, I went to practice every day and just watched. There were days when I woke up and didn't feel like doing it anymore. I'd cry myself to sleep. But deep in my heart,

I knew I could make it. I'd been through a lot of adversity before and knew that God had used those experiences to strengthen my faith in Him. Eventually, my injury became such an opportunity.

During my basketball career, I've suffered other injuries, like a torn meniscus and a torn achilles. When I faced those tough times, it would have been easier to give up. But no matter what the circumstance, I have a strong desire to remain loyal to myself, to my family, to my teams, and to our fans. Most importantly, I want to be loyal to my values and loyal to God. I represent Him in everything I do.

The foundation for my loyalty to biblical values started with my parents. I received even more preparation for life at the University of Tennessee from head coach Pat Summitt. Some have called her the "John Wooden of women's basketball." Not surprisingly, she talked about Coach Wooden often and shared his character-building principles with us.

Coach Summitt wanted us to be more than just basketball players. Most coaches recruit players to play basketball and do well in school. But to her, it was also about being active in the community and preparing us to be better once we left school.

From everything I've seen and read, Coach Wooden was the same way. He had a power about him. It was not a demanding presence, but even through just a smile, his spirit shined through. Yes, he had incredible success on the basketball court, but most people now talk about his character.

One story that stands out took place when he first got to UCLA in 1948. Coach Wooden had been led to believe that there would be a new basketball facility built by the time that contract ran out. But it didn't happen right away. Many coaches today would have left under those circumstances, yet Coach Wooden showed amazing integrity and loyalty to those who hired him.

In *Coach Wooden One-on-One,* he talked about how his teams practiced in "the old barn" and how he swept the floor every day before practice to clear off the dirt. The Bruins didn't even have their own home court throughout those early years and played in different arenas all around town.

That's the kind of integrity and character that I want people to see in my life. I've played all over the world in many different countries and with many different teams. When I leave those places, I don't know if I'll ever see those people again. So I want them to remember that I had a certain kind of strength about me and that I lived by my Christian principles. Whether I'm playing in Korea, Russia, Turkey or right here in the United States, my faithfulness to my values boils down to one huge question posed by Coach Wooden: Will I compromise my integrity when temptation is great?

Esther was a brave woman in the Bible that had to answer that same question. An orphaned Jewish woman, Esther was chosen by the Persian king Xerxes to be his queen. When one of the king's men plotted to destroy the Jews, she was warned by her cousin Mordecai, who told her she was the only one who could stop this from happening.

At that point, Esther could have easily turned her back on Mordecai and her own people. She could have said, "No, I'm fine. I'm here in the temple. I don't need any help." But instead, she took a stand and risked her own life in order to save the Jewish people.

In Esther 4:14, Mordecai suggested to Esther that perhaps she had been raised up by God "for such a time as this." But that wouldn't have mattered if she had allowed fear and selfishness to compromise her beliefs.

In the basketball realm, I look to Coach Wooden as an example of someone who never caved to the pressure of compromise. His example teaches that when you stay true to your values, there's nothing nagging at you. When you know what you're doing is right, you have peace.

WOODEN'S WISDOM

I wanted my players to become men of integrity. When we have integrity, we are not going to do anything that will be demeaning to anybody else, either on or off the court. And with integrity, we will never consider letting our teammates down.

TRAINING TIME

1. How have you responded in the past when you were tempted to cut corners and compromise your beliefs?

2. Reflect on Coach Wooden's question: "Will I compromise my integrity when temptation is great?"

3. What are some practical ways you can stay loyal to biblical truths and God's purpose for your life?

PRAYER

Father, thank You for giving me a purpose and goal for my life. Fill me with Your peace as I remain loyal to You and Your plan for me. Help me to avoid compromising my integrity and beliefs when temptation is great.

Tamika Catchings is an All-Star forward with the WNBA's Indiana Fever. She was an All-American while playing for the University of Tennessee and was part of the unde-feated 1998 national championship team. Catchings has also won two Olympic gold medals with the USA women's basketball team in Athens (2004) and Beijing (2008).

8

Be Prepared

BY GARY CUNNINGHAM

Former NCAA Forward and Head Coach, UCLA

---

*I must have the drive to develop my abilities and become
the best I can be so that I'll be ready.*
JOHN WOODEN

"Failure to prepare is preparing to fail." I can hear Coach Wooden saying those words as if it were yesterday. And it wasn't just some phrase he quoted to motivate his players and assistant coaches. Preparation was his way; it permeated every aspect of his life. And, in return, he taught us how to be prepared in our own lives, even beyond basketball.

From 1959 to 1962, I was privileged to play for Coach Wooden, and later I accepted an opportunity to coach on his staff for the last 10 years of his tenure at UCLA. Those experiences gave me the unique perspective of seeing his legendary preparation from both sides of the chalkboard. He was a stickler for details—I remember that so vividly.

The coaching staff would spend two hours planning and organizing the practice every morning. Coach Wooden had blocks of time—usually 5 to 10 minute segments—that were set aside for the drills. He kept a notebook of every practice that showed the sequence of preparation. He would use the notebook to back-track from the first game and discuss when we needed to put in things like the zone press attack and when we would work on fundamentals like jump balls.

Coach Wooden believed that if you did the right things during the week at practice, it would work out on the weekend when you played the games. Maybe that's why he never talked about winning. His last words in the locker room before the team took the floor were always, "Do the best you can. That's all you can ask of yourself. And only you know if you did the best you can."

That, of course, reverts back to the top of his Pyramid of Success. But it also speaks to Coach Wooden's dedicated view of preparation. He believed it didn't matter what the other team was doing. As long as his players were prepared to execute the game plan, good things would happen. That might not always mean winning, but in his opinion, doing one's best was the true gauge of success.

Preparation was also important for those players who didn't get as much playing time. Coach Wooden's philosophy was to play seven or eight players until games were won or lost. He was very up-front about that, but some of the players who were star players in high school and now were sitting on the bench found it difficult to understand. Coach Wooden always told them how much they were helping the team with their role in practice, but he also told them to be prepared. "Make sure you're ready," he would say, "because if you get that chance, you need to take advantage of it."

Later in my life, I found that principle of preparedness to be true. Because of the preparation I learned from Coach Wooden, I was able to take advantage of many great opportunities, including two seasons as head coach at UCLA from 1977 to 1979 and 29 years as an athletic director. Throughout each of those tenures, I did my best to prepare for whatever challenges might come my way. Whenever I experienced something new, I reflected upon the experience and filed it away for future reference. Ultimately, preparation meant following Coach Wooden's advice and developing my abilities to become the best I could be.

His example drove me to excel on the basketball court, and it inspired me to earn my doctorate in educational administration. I've learned from Coach Wooden's life that the only way to achieve greatness is through preparation.

WOODEN'S WISDOM

If I'm prepared, perhaps my chance will come. But if I'm not primed, I'll miss my opportunity, and it isn't likely to come again. I have to think as if I'm only going to get one shot, so I must be ready.

TRAINING TIME

1. How does the principle of being prepared at all times apply to your spiritual life?

2. Read 2 Timothy 2:20-22. According to these verses, what steps can you take to be prepared for the work God has for you?

3. Read 2 Timothy 4:1-3. According to these verses, how often should you be prepared to do the work God has for you?

PRAYER

Father, I want to be prepared at all times to do Your work and follow Your plan . Help me to have the discipline to grow in my faith daily, so I will be ready to give You my best when You call me off the bench to play for You.

Gary Cunningham is the former athletic director of the University of California at Santa Barbara. He played basketball for UCLA from 1959-62 and was part of the program's first-ever appearance in a Final Four (1962). He served as an assistant under Coach Wooden for 10 years and later led the Bruins to a 50-8 record as the head coach from 1977-79.

9

The Hard Way

BY STEVE ALFORD

Head Coach, Men's Basketball, University of New Mexico

There is no substitute for hard work.

JOHN WOODEN

Every time I went to practice, I would see Coach Wooden's picture hanging on the wall. It was the 1970s and my dad, Sam Alford, was the head basketball coach at Martinsville High School in Martinsville, Indiana, where Wooden was a three-time all-state basketball star and a key member of the 1927 state championship team.

Even in elementary school, I was the stereotypical gym rat. Every chance I got, I was in the Glenn Curtis Memorial Gymnasium shooting free throws, practicing dribbling techniques, running layup drills, or perfecting my jump shot. My daily routine was as consistent as the presence of Coach Wooden in that gym.

Back then I was inspired by Coach Wooden's success, and it made me want to play at the collegiate level and win a national championship as well. Although I didn't realize it at the time, my penchant for hard work was in some ways an extension of the kind of player and leader that Coach Wooden was.

It wasn't until I took my first coaching job at Manchester University in 1991 that Coach Wooden had his biggest impact on me. That's when I was truly able to appreciate the way he lived out his faith. He accomplished something in our game that will likely never be duplicated. Coach Wooden achieved greatness not by taking shortcuts but by leading with integrity and by teaching and modeling hard work.

In his book *Pyramid of Success*, I learned about the importance of hard work (or "industriousness," as Coach Wooden would say) from the personal examples he shared during that amazing run at UCLA. Each year, he only took a couple of weeks off before diving back into his job by researching aspects of the game, talking with other coaches, reading and doing detailed planning. He wanted his team to be the best the right way, and that meant him working hard to prepare them to succeed.

That's important because the opportunity to bend the rules is a serious temptation for many coaches. It's easier to succeed by taking short cuts. Now, I want to win as much as anybody, but I made a commitment a long time ago to coach with integrity and, like Coach Wooden, to do it the right way.

I've also been inspired by Coach Wooden's principle to "make each day a masterpiece" and steadily push my players through individual development. If I can convince my players that they can improve every day—whether that means practicing for one hour or three hours—then it's been a successful day.

This concept of hard work stands true in our spiritual lives as well. In Proverbs 14:23, Solomon writes, "There is profit in all hard work." You have to work awfully hard to live out your faith. It's not easy living with integrity in today's compromising world, but Coach Wooden has proved that it can be done. He not only worked hard as a coach and a player but also made his faith a priority.

Coach Wooden's legacy shows that there is more to life than success as measured by sports achievements and championships.

He has lived by the promise of Colossians 3:23-24, "Whatever you do, do it enthusiastically, as something done for the Lord and not for men, knowing that you will receive the reward of an inheritance from the Lord—you serve the Lord Christ."

We don't work hard for the sake of achieving our goals; we work hard to please God. And the result is something eternal—something that will last much longer than plaques and trophies.

WOODEN'S WISDOM

Most people have a tendency to look for shortcuts or at least for the easiest way to complete any given task. If we only put out a minimum effort we might get by in some situations, but in the long run we won't fully develop the talents that lie within us.

TRAINING TIME

1. How does hard work bring about integrity and improvement?

2. Is it easy or hard to live out your faith in daily life?

3. Read Colossians 3:23-24. What are some areas of your life you need to work hard at for God and not for man?

PRAYER

Father, help me to realize that everything I do needs to be for You and no one else. Help me to work hard at every task You give me so I may have integrity and gain success in Your eyes.

Steve Alford is the men's basketball coach at the University of New Mexico, where he has led the Lobos to a pair of Mountain West Conference championships (2009 and 2010). Previously, Alford spent eight seasons as the head coach at Iowa and four seasons at Missouri State. Previously, Alford spent eight seasons as the head coach at Iowa, four seasons at Missouri State, and four seasons at Manchester College.

The Good Fight

BY SHERRI COALE

Head Coach, Women's Basketball, University of Oklahoma

Fight is a determined effort to do the very best we can do.

JOHN WOODEN

It was probably an odd choice for a fifth-grader. But at the annual book fair, I bought a little paperback called *They Call Me Coach*. It was my first year playing basketball at Sunset Elementary School in Healdton, Oklahoma, and I wanted to learn everything I could about the sport. Even then, I was driven and determined to do my best.

That book was my first introduction to Coach Wooden. In it, I learned that his incredible success wasn't measured in championships. It was all about the intangible things and the influence you have on people. Success was measured by kindness, honesty and integrity. In other words, anybody could be extraordinary.

Coach Wooden never talked about shooting a million shots a day or being 6′ 8″ or any of those things that I did not have and could not control. He was able to build a dynasty at UCLA based on the things on which every individual has an opportunity to develop and excel. He taught that success could be a reality for anyone.

So, early on as a player, I attached myself to that book and all of the inspirational quotes. Coach Wooden was a former English teacher and he loved poetry, especially the simple rhymes that were easy to remember. They held great meaning for me. I wrote them down and pasted them in my locker and in the front of my notebook. I carried them with me in my gym bag. Those lessons set the tone for my playing career.

Even now as a coach, Wooden's principles have been at the forefront of everything I do. I remember combing through his books when we were building the program at Oklahoma, and I still use many of his principles today, especially the Pyramid of Success. Of all the Pyramid's timeless teachings, the principle of fight has always resonated with me—going all the way back to my days as a tenacious grade-school point guard.

Fight is that one thing that serves as the axis for our team. If we fight hard, then we never have anything to be ashamed of. It is one of the important things that we can control. Talent and luck come and go, but when you have fight, you give yourself a chance to win—even if you're less talented. And even if you are talented, fight gives you the chance to be the best and stay there.

Fight is the one thing you can always feel good about. If you fight, regardless of the outcome of a game, when it's finished, you have a right to feel proud about what you've just done. In basketball terms, Coach Wooden describes fight as "diving to the floor for loose balls." That reminds me of Lauren Shoush, a student who played for me for four years at the University of Oklahoma. She made our team extraordinary, because every time the ball was on the floor, she dove after it.

When Coach Wooden talks about "sprinting to fill the lane on a fast break," I immediately think about LaNeishea

Caufield from our 2002 team. I could count on her to fill the lane and find a way to get to the rim when Stacey Dales had the ball so she could be in position for a pass.

Wooden also describes fight as "digging in, gritting our teeth, standing our ground." Those words speak of the times our team won when we were far from being the odds-on favorites. In 2002, we fought our way to the Final Four and defeated Duke before facing Connecticut in the championship game. In 2004, we ran the table by winning four straight games and claiming the Big 12 tournament title.

But fight transcends what happens inside the boundaries of a basketball floor; it also plays an important role in our personal battles. Jamie Talbert-Wyrick was our center during the 2001 and 2002 seasons. After graduating, she faced ovarian and thyroid cancer, but she gritted her teeth and stood her ground and made it through. Her former teammates fought alongside her and helped her through her biggest challenge. Today, Jamie is cancer-free.

Fight is a way of life. It's how we thrive. And it has a direct correlation to our spiritual lives. In 2 Timothy 4:7, the apostle Paul writes, "I have fought the good fight, I have finished the race, I have kept the faith."

When you talk about gritting your teeth and standing your ground, nowhere is it more important than in your daily Christian walk. Sometimes we are faced with making a decision that isn't easy but is absolutely necessary. That requires fight. Coach Wooden demonstrated and taught the principle of fight to his players, but he never did so simply to help them win games. Instead, he taught them the principle of fight to help develop their character.

Like Coach Wooden, I hope to show my teams and others within my sphere of influence that living every aspect of life with that determined effort is the key to being extraordinary.

WOODEN'S WISDOM

On the basketball court, fight is measured by hustle; diving to the floor for loose balls, sprinting to fill a lane on a fast break, taking a charge, picking up a missed defensive assignment or stealing the ball from an opposing player. It's digging in, gritting our teeth, standing our ground.

TRAINING TIME

1. How is Coach Wooden's definition of fight different than what you have heard in the past?

2. Read 2 Timothy 4:7-8. What is the fight that Paul describes here?

3. How can you incorporate "fight" into the spiritual challenges and decisions you face daily?

PRAYER

Father, thank You for the "good fight." Help me to stand against temptations and challenges that I face daily and stand up for my faith. Help me to have fight in my spiritual life!

Sherri Coale is the head women's basketball coach at the University of Oklahoma where she has led the Sooners to four Big 12 tournament championships and six regular season titles. As of the end of the 2009-2010 season, Coale's teams have made the NCAA tournament 11 times including three appearances in the Final Four. Coale is also a four-time Big 12 Coach of the Year.

The Honest Truth

BY JERRY COLANGELO

Executive Director, USA Basketball

Honesty is doing the things that we know are right and not giving into the temptation to do the things that we know are wrong.

JOHN WOODEN

Nowhere have I seen greater respect for a former coach than from those athletes who played for Coach Wooden. I saw it in those great UCLA teams of the late '60s with players like Gail Goodrich and Keith Erickson. As we assembled the first team for the Chicago Bulls, we took Erickson from the San Francisco Warriors in the '66 expansion draft. Two years later, I selected Goodrich to start for the Phoenix Suns. Both players could get the job done on the court, but it was their time spent under Wooden's tutelage and the way he taught them to be team players despite their individual talent that made them attractive.

Being around those players, and meeting others along the way, I saw how Coach Wooden influenced them. They respected Coach Wooden because he had the utmost integrity and rock-solid principles. These values transferred over to his players and made them the type of recruits that I wanted on my team.

Coach Wooden's faith also impressed me, because in those early years I was being transformed in my personal faith in Jesus Christ. I held up Coach Wooden as a role model of a person who had it all together. Over the years, I've tried my best to model Coach Wooden's principles in whatever circumstances I've faced.

The principle that has played the most important role in my life is that one's word is one's bond. I've learned through Coach Wooden's example that leading with honesty goes a long way. On the other hand, "Dishonesty—no matter the reason—destroys our credibility, ruins our reputation and costs us our self-respect." Coach Wooden's words, as chronicled in *Pyramid of Success*, have always served as a somber reminder of how important it is to honor one's word.

For me, that principle held true when I was asked to take over as the national director of USA Basketball. The program was in shambles after the 2004 Summer Olympics. The U.S. Men's Team performed below expectations and struggled to a bronze medal finish at those Games.

I agreed to take on the task, but with certain provisions. One of those provisions was total autonomy. I needed complete control over the budget and in choosing the coaches and players. The U.S. Olympic Committee agreed to my terms, and from there all I really had at my disposal to sell the NBA athletes was the vision and my passion.

Kobe Bryant, LeBron James, Dwyane Wade, Dwight Howard, Chris Paul, Carmelo Anthony, and on down the line—I didn't talk to anyone who turned down the offer. I asked them to check their egos at the door. They did. I told them it would be the greatest experience of their lives. They all said it was.

The media dubbed that collection of NBA All-Stars the "Redeem Team." After a disappointing third-place finish at the 2006 World Championships, the U.S. National Team took gold at the FIBA Americas Championship. Then, at the 2008 Summer Olympic Games in Beijing, China, the team went undefeated in seven games. As a result, the players and coaches left with more than just a gold medal. They took home a great feeling in knowing they shared something special on an international stage.

But that success didn't happen on a whim. The respect I had earned from those players was built over 40 years working in the world of professional sports. I've been involved with the construction of stadiums, arenas and theaters worth billions of dollars. I've signed multi-million-dollar contracts with a host of players. My word was my bond and my handshake was good enough for most of them.

Unfortunately, honesty and integrity seem to be dying character traits, and that makes me sad. People today are hesitant to take someone simply at their word or with a handshake. The reason for this is because respect and trust are earned over a period of time. It just doesn't happen overnight, and you can't ordain it. King Solomon spoke that truth in Proverbs 11:3: "The integrity of the upright guides them, but the perversity of the treacherous destroys them."

I was especially blessed to know Coach Wooden because he spent much of his life striving to be like Jesus. For me, that meant living a life marked by honesty and devoid of compromise. That's the kind of life that commands respect and, more importantly, opens the door to share our faith with others.

WOODEN'S WISDOM

Honesty must occur at all times, in both thought and action.
Honest people stay on the narrow way, regardless of the consequences.
If we are honest, our integrity will not allow us to compromise ever.
Honest people don't lie to others, to themselves or to God.

TRAINING TIME

1. Who is someone in your life that you respect because of his or her honesty and integrity?

2. Read Proverbs 11:3. What are some areas of your life in which you need to show more honesty and integrity?

3. How can having honesty and integrity help you stay faithful to the tasks God has given you?

PRAYER

Father, thank You for the godly example of the others in my life. Help me to live my life with honesty and integrity and be faithful to the tasks You have given me, whether they are big or small.

Jerry Colangelo is the national director of USA Basketball and a member of the Naismith Memorial Basketball Hall of Fame. He is the co-founder and former owner of multiple professional sports teams, including the NBA's Chicago Bulls and Phoenix Suns and the MLB's Arizona Diamondbacks.

Giving Up Control

BY JOE GIRARDI
Manager, New York Yankees

God is either in control or He isn't. I believe He is.
JOHN WOODEN

Throughout my baseball career, I've come to realize that God has always been in control. But I haven't always thought that way. When I was 13 years old, my mother was diagnosed with cancer and given three months to live. But instead, she lived six more years. During that time, I thought I was playing baseball to give her something to live for.

I was playing in Winston-Salem, North Carolina, when she passed away. I was doing really well for a while, but then all of a sudden it hit me: I didn't know why I was playing. So I came home to Northwestern University in Illinois, where at the time I was dating Kim, now my wife of 20 years. She led me to the Lord and helped me realize that God had given me a gift. That's why I was playing.

As I grew in my faith, I began to better understand the concept of God's providence. So many times I thought I was in a certain place for the rest of my baseball career—like when I played for the Chicago Cubs or for the Colorado Rockies—but then God would have different plans. Finally, I went to New York where, in the beginning, it was very difficult for me to adjust to the intense media scrutiny and high expectations. That first season in 1996, of course, turned out to be an amazing journey, as the Yankees captured the World Series title.

Sometimes we don't understand why God puts us places, but over time we can see that there is a reason for everything He does. We understand that He is in charge. So many of the things that have happened in my life wouldn't have been what I would have picked. But God put me where He wanted me, not necessarily where I wanted to go.

This truth became even more real when I first met Coach Wooden. At the time, I was a bench coach with the Yankees. We were playing in Anaheim during the 2005 season, and Coach Wooden was in manager Joe Torre's office. Before meeting him, I knew that he was a great coach. I remember watching some of his UCLA championship teams when I was younger. He was a legend.

But when I listened to Coach Wooden talk for the few minutes we had with him, it was his faith that spoke volumes. That's what really intrigued me. It created a desire in me to learn more about him. I read up on him and quickly learned that he was a man of his word and his commitment. It made me admire him even more.

I especially love the story of how Coach Wooden ended up at UCLA. At the time he was pursuing a job at Minnesota, but when a phone call didn't take place because a snowstorm took out the phone lines, he instead took the job at UCLA. Despite the fact that he wanted to stay closer to home and his Midwestern roots, Coach Wooden ultimately trusted God for his future and moved to Southern California. Even later in his career when he wanted to take a job at Purdue, his alma mater, he remained a man of his word and stayed true to the path God had chosen for him.

That story confirmed what I already felt in my spirit—that God is in charge of our lives. I think about all of the people Coach Wooden touched because he understood that principle. When you come to that conclusion, you don't stop acting on faith. Certainly that's something Coach Wooden had firmly grasped, and it's a truth that has become more evident in my life.

When I realized that God had given me a gift, I also realized that with that gift, He had given me a platform. If we have faith and understand what Jesus is all about—that love is the greatest commandment, as He teaches us in Matthew 22:37-39—then our actions will follow suit. We'll want to be there for people. We'll want to do good things for people. We'll want to give up control of our personal desires and reach out to those who are struggling—very much like Jesus did.

As I've learned from Coach Wooden's example, it takes a strong measure of faith to be able to walk each day in love. It's the kind of faith that allows us to trust God's plan for our lives and let Him take control, no matter where He might lead.

WOODEN'S WISDOM

I also believe that [God] delegates certain responsibilities to us. This does not mean that we earn His favor. We can't work our way into His good graces. But we do have some responsibility in the successful development of our faith. Faith without works is dead. Likewise, works without faith are also worthless.

TRAINING TIME

1. Have you ever been through a time when you questioned why God put you in a certain place?

2. How did God reveal to you that He was in control and you were exactly where He wanted you to be?

3. What is one area of your life in which you need to give God complete control?

PRAYER

Father, thank You for taking control of my life and placing me exactly where You want me to be. Help me to see Your plan for my life and trust You with the future.

Joe Girardi is the manager of the New York Yankees and a former 15-year veteran catcher. He has been a part of four World Series championship teams—three as a player (1996, 1998, 1999) and one as a manager (2009)—all as a member of the Yankees.

13

Count on Me

BY RUTH RILEY

WNBA Forward, San Antonio Silver Stars

When we are reliable, others know that they can depend on us.
JOHN WOODEN

Basketball, like most team sports, isn't really about talent as much as it's about trust. You have to trust the people you're on the court with, and they have to trust you. It takes mutual trust between all the players as the team works toward the common goal.

Coach Wooden brilliantly applied this principle to his Pyramid of Success. He described the concept as "reliability," or, as some might refer to it, "dependability." It refers to a consistent level of trustworthiness that we show to those around us.

Coach Wooden heavily influenced many of my coaches, who in turn taught me his philosophy on sports and life. In his Pyramid of Success, I love the way he used building construction to illustrate his definition of success. All of the blocks are bound together with mortar; a paste-like substance that fills the gaps and makes the structure sound and strong. What an amazing picture of a team! When players can rely on each other, the team chemistry is sound. But it takes great effort to be reliable. It's not an easy task, and because of that, not everyone chooses to do it.

In my basketball career, I've played various roles within a team. Two that come to mind are my role as a starter at Notre Dame, where I was expected to produce the majority of points and rebounds, and my role as a bench player, which I have filled more recently in my career with the San Antonio Stars.

In college, my teammates found me to be reliable on the offensive end of the court. As a 6' 5" center, I was able to shoot a high percentage in the post and pull down offensive boards. My height also gave me an advantage on the defensive side, where I made a difference with blocked shots and rebounds. But I didn't take my game for granted. I was determined to be a dependable teammate and try my best to perform at a high level.

This was especially true during my senior year when I won the Naismith Award and was named Associated Press Player of the Year. While I was happy to be recognized, I was much more concerned about our team goals that culminated at the 2001 NCAA championship game. Playing against Purdue, we were trailing 66-64 late in the game. I got the ball and put up the game-tying shot.

With the game still tied, I got another chance to put our team ahead but was fouled while shooting. I made both shots, and we won the national championship 68-66. Coach Muffet McGraw joked afterward that on the last sequence she called the same play the team had been running all season: "Get the ball to Ruth."

Playing in the WNBA has been a bit different. I've had my chances to start and be a major contributor, but recently as the league has grown and players have improved, I've found that sometimes the best way I can be reliable is to come off the bench and encourage our starters or give the team a boost of energy. Reliability has changed for me. It requires being consistent in practice and challenging my teammates to give their best by demonstrating hard work and, occasionally, becoming a vocal, veteran leader.

As I've found throughout my career and my life, reliability takes time and effort. In today's fast-paced world, those are often hard to find. That's because time and effort are tied to qualities that are even rarer: selflessness and sacrifice.

Reliability takes sacrifice because of the many things that can distract us from consistency. Being there for someone means focusing on an individual or circumstance and taking on the responsibility of seeing things through. In a team dynamic, this might mean spending extra time working on drills or taking the time to build relationships off the court. It's doing whatever is necessary to make the team better. That takes a great deal of sacrifice.

Reliability also requires a high level of selflessness. Unfortunately, a lot of athletes just play for individual goals. If all of the players have that mentality, no one can be a good leader. It's very difficult to work together and find chemistry when there's not a leader who cares about the team and is willing to be selfless and reliable.

Jesus personified reliability. When He walked the earth, He was both selfless and sacrificial. His disciples knew they could depend on Him. When they were distressed during the storm, Jesus calmly arose from His sleep on the boat and told the winds to be still.

His disciples, however, weren't always so faithful. When Jesus pleaded with them to stay awake and pray with Him in the Garden of Gethsemane just hours before His crucifixion, they were too weak. They didn't have the strength to sacrifice of themselves and be dependable for their Savior.

Coach Wooden once said that when we display reliability, "People can bet the farm on us and still be able to sleep at night." The same is true when it comes to our relationship with Christ. He is the model of reliability. One of my favorite Bible promises in Hebrews 13:5 states this very fact: "He Himself has said, I will never leave you or forsake you."

Not only does this challenge me to be more reliable in my spiritual walk, but it also motivates me to be—just like Coach Wooden was throughout his life—a consistent model of reliability, faith-fulness and trustworthiness to my teammates, my friends, my family and anyone God places in my path.

WOODEN'S WISDOM

[When we are reliable, others] know that we will make the effort to do our best, whatever the situation might be. They know we won't run, cower or become paralyzed by fear. They have learned to count on our consistency and trustworthiness. We'll still be there making the effort to do our best long after the weaker ones have faded. People can bet the farm on us and still be able to sleep at night. Reliability earns the respect of those around us.

TRAINING TIME

1. Are you showing a consistent level of trust to those around you?

2. Why does it take great effort to be reliable?

3. In what areas of your life do you need to become selfless and sacrificial in order to model Jesus' example of reliability?

PRAYER

Jesus, thank You for Your example of selflessness that ultimately led You to the cross to die for me. Thank You for Your promise to never leave me or forsake me. Help me to model Your example of reliability to my teammates, friends and family.

Ruth Riley is a WNBA center with the San Antonio Silver Stars. She was previously a member of the Detroit Shock where she was a two-time championship series MVP. Riley was an Olympic gold medalist at the 2004 Athens Games and a two-time All-American at Notre Dame. She led the Irish to the 2001 National Championship and was named Most Outstanding Player at that year's Final Four.

14

Do As I Do

BY LORENZO ROMAR
Head Coach, Men's Basketball, University of Washington

A leader's most powerful ally is his or her own example.
JOHN WOODEN

By far, Coach Wooden was the most impressive man I ever met in my entire life. There was something about his authentic leadership that inherently caused others to follow . . . and I've been one of his followers since I was young.

Growing up in Compton during the late '60s and early '70s, I was like most kids from Southern California. It was all about Bruins basketball. My first introduction to the program was the 1968 national championship team that featured Lew Alcindor, Lucius Allen and Mike Warren. I watched all of UCLA's games on TV and was captivated by the interviews with Coach Wooden.

My star-struck obsession drove me to take the hour-and-a-half bus ride to Pauley Pavilion on weekends, where I would try to catch some playing time on the court. My primary objective was to spot Coach Wooden and some of his players.

In the spring of 1978, I had just finished playing two years of basketball at Cerritos Community College. I was on my way home from the University of Washington, my fourth official visit as part of the recruiting process. I really liked Washington more than the other schools, but I still had a tough decision to make. As I walked to the LAX baggage claim, I was surprised to see Coach Wooden a hundred feet ahead of me.

I knew I had to say hello and felt motivated to ask him where I should go to school. I caught up to him and introduced myself. He was very gracious. When I told him what universities were offering me a scholarship, he politely said, "If you have a chance to play for Marv Harshman, that's hard to turn down." His brief but convincing advice was partly the reason I chose to play for the Huskies, the team I now coach.

Even after that meeting, I didn't truly understand Coach Wooden's unique leadership qualities—at least not until 1993, when, as assistant coach at UCLA, I was able to spend time in his home and sit at his feet, so to speak. Our staff spent three hours talking basketball with Coach as he masterfully intertwined life's lessons. It was then that I learned that what set Coach apart were the rare qualities of humility, integrity and a serving heart. He didn't expect others to do what he couldn't or wouldn't do. He set the example for others to follow.

Three years later, when I took my first head-coaching job at Pepperdine, I took my staff to spend time with Coach Wooden. Something interesting happened when I got back home. He called to tell me that one of my assistant coaches had dropped some change in the couch.

"I want to get that back to him," Coach Wooden said.

"Oh, Coach, don't worry about it," I replied.

"No, I want to make sure he gets it," he insisted.

I again told him not to worry about it. After all, it was only 75 cents. Two months later, Coach Wooden was scheduled to speak at my basketball camp at Pepperdine. I picked him up, and when he got in the car, the first thing he handed me was the 75 cents.

That was Coach Wooden's way—he was detailed in doing things right. He didn't need to teach a lesson about integrity. He lived it out and set a consistent example for those around him. It was authentic leadership that so many of us are still compelled to follow.

As someone who wants to model that kind of leadership, the biggest challenge I face is the ups and downs. The game of basketball can be very emotional. It's easy to get frustrated with constant pressures and stressful situations. All eyes are on the coach. When adversity comes, it's tempting to react a certain way. But I try to control myself. I want to be an example and handle life's challenges in a godly manner.

I'm reminded of a situation at Pepperdine when we had about 20 minutes left of practice and the volleyball team was scheduled to use the gym next. There was a maintenance person whose job was to pull up the baskets at a certain time in preparation for volleyball practice. On this particular day, the volleyball team wasn't quite ready, and I knew it. I decided to extend our practice by five minutes.

Without saying a word, the maintenance man started lifting the baskets during our practice. I wanted to say, "What in the world are you doing?" but I didn't. I could see the players looking at me, wondering how I was going to react.

So instead I said, "Hey, we're not quite done yet."

"It doesn't matter," the maintenance man rudely replied. "I'm putting the baskets up." I could see my team still looking at me. How would I respond to his belligerence?

"No, no. It's going to be fine," I calmly replied. "You can leave them down."

And he left them down.

It may not have seemed like a big thing at the time, but as the coach, how I dealt with such a confrontation sent a clear message to my players. In that moment, I didn't have to explain my actions. The team experienced firsthand how to properly deal with conflict.

It's with that same purpose that I try to live as a believer. I'm challenged by the words of the apostle Paul who wrote in 1 Corinthians 11:1, "Be imitators of me, as I also am of Christ." Paul was telling the church to follow his lead. He wasn't perfect, but he was going to try to live an example so the early Christians would have a point of reference for their faith journey.

I take Paul's words to heart. They remind me that I might be the only Bible that someone reads. And as I observed Coach Wooden live out God's Word without quoting Scripture, I came to understand that all believers are called to imitate Christ so that others will be compelled to not necessarily do as we say but do as we do.

That's authentic leadership.

WOODEN'S WISDOM

There is hypocrisy to the phrase, "Do as I say, not as I do." I refused to make demands on my boys that I wasn't willing to live out in my own life. . . . Leadership from a base of hypocrisy undermines respect, and if people don't respect you, they won't willingly follow you.

TRAINING TIME

1. How does the world's view of leadership differ from God's view of leadership?

2. What are some character traits of authentic leadership that you can incorporate into your daily life?

3. Read Ephesians 5:1. How is Jesus the ultimate example of authentic leadership?

PRAYER

*Father, help me to imitate You and follow Your example
of authentic leadership. Help me to live with humility,
integrity and a servant's heart as I set an example and
lead others around me.*

Lorenzo Romar is the men's basketball coach at the University of Washington, where he has led the Huskies to five NCAA Tournament appearances. Romar was also an assistant coach on UCLA's 1995 national championship team. As a player, he enjoyed five years in the NBA with Golden State, Milwaukee, and Detroit.

15

The Real Deal

BY PAT WILLIAMS
Senior Vice President, Orlando Magic

Integrity in its simplest form is purity of intention.
JOHN WOODEN

One of Coach Wooden's former student managers once told me, "Here's the deal with John Wooden. There was only one of him. The John Wooden on the practice floor was the same John Wooden on the campus. And the John Wooden on the campus was the same John Wooden at home."

Coach Wooden remained the same, no matter the circumstances or environment. He was consistent. His walk and his talk matched up.

Coach Wooden was a model of integrity, but like so many others, I didn't come to understand that fact until much later in life. My first encounter with Coach was in 1962. I was a senior and the catcher on Wake Forest's baseball team. Our basketball team, led by Len Chappell, Billy Packer and Coach Bones McKinney, had advanced to the Final Four that year, and so had Coach Wooden's UCLA team. It was his first trip in the 14 years he had been coaching the Bruins.

The NCAA still had a consolation game in those days—a game open only to the losers in the early stages of the competition. Wake Forest lost to Ohio State in the national semi-final and faced UCLA, who had been defeated by eventual champion Cincinnati. Up until that point I didn't know much about Coach Wooden, as UCLA was just emerging onto the national stage. I remember wondering, *Are they any good? How did they get here? What's the story with them?*

Wake Forest won the game, but it was to be Coach Wooden's last NCAA tournament loss for a long, long time. At the time of this writing, more than three decades after his retirement, Coach Wooden remains the most successful coach in college basketball history. His UCLA teams scaled unprecedented heights that have been unmatched in more than three decades. During that period, Wooden had 88 consecutive victories, 10 NCAA championships and 38 consecutive NCAA tournament victories.

Coach Wooden retired following the 1975 season, and the world somewhat lost track of him for about 20 years. He was in his mid-eighties before he re-emerged as a national teaching figure and people finally heard his voice. Coach Wooden was such a humble man. He didn't want to upstage other coaches, and he wasn't convinced that anybody would want to hear what he had to say.

When I began working in the NBA as a general manager, I would often run into Coach Wooden's former players and hear them talk about him. But some waited until retirement to share about his influence. Players like Bill Walton and Kareem Abdul-Jabbar did not begin to express themselves about Coach Wooden until much later in life. Now, all of Coach's life principles are registering with them in a big way.

But for the rest of us, Coach was rediscovered as a teacher. Thanks to that little blue book of wisdom he wrote called *The Essential Wooden*, Coach became relevant again. That's the first time many of us really got a solid look at what Coach Wooden was all about. It was our initial glimpse into the mind and the heart of this man who epitomized integrity. And it made us hungry for more.

Coach's words of wisdom eventually inspired me to write a book called *How to Be Like Coach Wooden*. That book was a real adventure for me and launched my personal relationship with Wooden. I wrote him a letter asking for his blessing to pursue the project. He obliged and, as a result, I was blessed to be able to spend five or six evenings with him over a dinner or a breakfast during that time.

The book came out in 2006, and even now I'm just beginning to understand what a privilege it was to be immersed in his life. There may be many John Woodens out there in different fields, but let's face it: This man's coaching success and that great run at UCLA is a huge part of why we admire him. That's the door opener. But once you walk through the door, you come to see, respect and admire the rare qualities he possessed that went way beyond coaching. There are very few people in life who touch you like that.

Coach Wooden was one of the few people who, when you left his presence, you felt that you had been scrubbed with a cleansing detergent. You literally felt close to being purified after spending time with him. I found it took the better part of four or five days just to get my equilibrium back. It was an overwhelming experience. Very seldom do you have the opportunity to know that you have been in the presence of greatness—not just accomplishment, but also a truly great person.

After spending time with Coach Wooden, you wanted to take your own game as a human being to another level. You did not want to disappoint him—you wanted him to be proud of you. Even though I lived 3,000 miles away from Coach, he was there in my life every day. I *wanted* to please him. He owed me nothing, and I owed him nothing, but I wanted to please him.

Doesn't that sound a lot like the way people felt after they were in the presence of Jesus? It should be no surprise that Christ was Coach Wooden's example. That's whom he looked to. He was never bombastic about that, but his faith was very real to him.

Even more exemplary is the way Jesus modeled integrity. In the first days of His ministry, He was out in the desert, and the devil was pounding on Him and asking Him to do all sorts of tricks. But Jesus didn't succumb. He simply quoted Scripture and stood firm. Jesus didn't fall. If He had compromised His integrity at that point, we wouldn't be talking about Him today.

In our society, there's a sense that to be successful in life, you've got to cut corners. You've got to shave the edges, and you can't operate straight down the middle. But I've come to believe that you can be successful and honest at the same time. You can be successful and maintain integrity for your entire life.

Coach Wooden proved it.

WOODEN'S WISDOM
Purity of intention is really a reflection of the heart. . . .
The heart of a person with integrity always wants to do what's right,
once he or she is sure what "right" is.

TRAINING TIME

1. Who has been a model of integrity in your life?

2. Would people say that you are the same person at school, work, practice, and at home?

3. Read Matthew 4:1-11. How did Jesus model integrity?

PRAYER

Father, thank You for being the ultimate example of integrity. Help me to maintain a life of integrity no matter where I am at or who I am around.

Pat Williams is the senior vice president of the NBA's Orlando Magic, a bestselling author and a popular motivational speaker. As general manager of the Philadelphia 76ers, he helped build the 1983 NBA Championship team that featured NBA Hall of Fame inductees Julius Erving and Moses Malone.

16

One Purpose

BY RALPH DROLLINGER

Former NCAA Center, UCLA, and Founder, Capitol Ministries

*Intentness is the ability to resist temptation and to avoid
rabbit trails of distraction.*

JOHN WOODEN

Coach Wooden was never a fan of the slam-dunk. So it's ironic that the first time I met him was right after I dislocated my finger by dunking a basketball on a stiff, metal rim.

During the summer before my senior year in high school, I attended one of Coach Wooden's basketball camps at Pacific Palisades. Already close to 7′ 0″ in height, I got involved in a pickup game on an outside court and injured my finger. Coach Wooden was the one that came on the scene and restored my joint to its proper position.

A little over a year later, I got a phone call to play for Coach Wooden at UCLA. I was told that I was one of three players they had selected to recruit throughout the entire country. Other colleges begged me to play at their school, but with Coach Wooden it was just the opposite. It was an honor that he selected me to play for him.

During my freshman year on the team, I started to understand what made Coach Wooden so special. He was more intent than anyone else I had ever been around. He had ferocity
in preparing his teams to be their best. Every day at practice,
Coach had a formula that he orchestrated and conducted, and
we followed that format.

His intentness was the key to getting us to play together
and run according to his philosophy. Coach was intent on
molding his players to his style. If you didn't play his way, you
didn't play.

We had to sacrifice a lot of things in order to be intent on
one purpose. When we played on those national championship
teams, we had two weeks at the beginning of the school year to
get our feet and bodies into condition, and then we started
practice. We missed Thanksgiving break because we were practicing. We missed Christmas with our families because of practice and tournaments. And when we went to the Final Four, we
missed Easter. We didn't go home until summer, because we
were so focused on basketball. But throughout that process,
Coach Wooden was able to harness the energy of 12 or 13 different players and focus them on one unified purpose.

Coach Wooden tapped into the same kind of focus that
drove the apostle Paul to sacrifice his life in order to spread the
gospel. In Philippians 3:12-14, he wrote:

> Not that I have already reached [the goal] or am al-
> ready fully mature, but I make every effort to take hold
> of it because I also have been taken hold of by Christ
> Jesus. Brothers, I do not consider myself to have taken
> hold of it. But one thing I do: forgetting what is be-
> hind and reaching forward to what is ahead, I pursue
> as my goal the prize promised by God's heavenly call in
> Christ Jesus.

Paul was intent on one thing: pursuing a relationship with God through His Son, Jesus, and sharing God's love with others along the way.

I can relate to Paul's sentiment. Since playing for Coach Wooden, I've learned to carry over the principle of intentness into spreading the gospel worldwide through Capitol Ministries. To achieve my goal of placing 200 ministries in 200 world capitals, I have to take all of my energy and focus it on that one purpose.

That is one of the greatest lessons I learned from Coach Wooden: being intent on one purpose and using your God-given abilities to achieve the goals He has placed before you. He will give you the "determination, stamina, and resolve" to "stay the course and go the distance."

WOODEN'S WISDOM

An intent person will stay the course and go the distance. He or she will concentrate on objectives with determination, stamina, and resolve. Intentness is the quality that won't permit us to quit, even when our goal is going to take a while to accomplish.

TRAINING TIME

1. What are some things in your life you are intent about?

2. Read Philippians 3:12-14. As Christians, what is the one goal we should be focused on?

3. In your own life, what is one thing God has called you to do, and how can you be intent about it?

PRAYER

Father, help me to avoid temptation and be intent on the path that You have chosen for me. Help me to have single-minded focus on the goals You have called me to accomplish.

Ralph Drollinger is the founder of Capitol Ministries, an organization that ministers to legislators in domestic and international capitals. He and his wife, Danielle, lead the ministry in Washington, D.C. Drollinger played for UCLA from 1972 to 1976 and was the first player in NCAA history to make four consecutive Final Four appearances.

17

Random Acts of Kindness

BY DENNY CRUM

Former Head Coach, Men's Basketball, University of Louisville

*Helping others in any way—with a smile,
a nod or a pat on the back—warms the heart.*

JOHN WOODEN

Treat people with kindness and play in the Final Four. Those were the two things I assumed I was supposed to do when I first took over as head coach of Louisville's basketball program in 1971. They seemed like natural responses after being an assistant coach under Coach Wooden.

My journey at UCLA started a few years earlier as a guard from nearby San Fernando. After two years at Los Angeles's Pierce College, I jumped at the chance to end my career playing for the Bruins.

In the fall of 1956, I was a junior transfer preparing for my first practice. I got dressed, taped and arrived at the court early. To my surprise, Coach Wooden was already there, using a broom and wet towel to sweep the floor. Here was a successful coach of a major college basketball program, and all I could think was, *Wow! This guy is mopping the floor?*

Once the entire team had arrived, Coach Wooden sat us down, told us to take off our shoes and socks, and then explained how to put them on properly to prevent blisters. I thought, *Holy mackerel! I've never seen anything like this!*

Coach Wooden was that way with everything, and his attention to detail was amazing. He had a 3″ x 5″ index card with all of the drills we were to do and how many minutes to spend on each. He was well organized and efficient. Even then, I knew I wanted to be a coach. Playing for Coach Wooden gave me an incredible opportunity to learn from the best.

After my senior season, I stayed as a coach for the freshman team. I eventually left to take the head coaching job at Pierce, but four years later I returned to UCLA as Coach Wooden's top assistant and lead recruiter. That's when I really saw how much preparation he put into his job. We'd spend 20 to 30 minutes a day evaluating the previous day's practice before we planned the next. He loved to teach, and watching him in action inspired me.

During my three years as Coach Wooden's assistant, I learned something much more important than how to teach the game of basketball. He taught me about the art of kindness and the joy of giving. I saw how he treated the secretaries and the coaches from other sports. They all looked up to him and respected him.

Something was different about Coach Wooden, and it showed up in the way that he interacted with others. Most days, assistant coach Gary Cunningham and I would walk with Coach to the village to have lunch at Hollis Johnson's place, a drug store that served sandwiches. The three of us would sit on milk cartons in the back of the establishment. Hollis would cook our meal, and sometimes Lakers star Jerry West, Hollis' fishing buddy, would stop by. We would sit and talk about life and basketball.

Everyone respected Coach for his success, but it was kindness that drew people to him. It felt good to share in those special moments. Coach Wooden influenced just about everything I did from that point on.

At Louisville, I inherited a team with several seniors, and we advanced to the Final Four. At the time, I guess I didn't know any better, but after winning three national championships in three years coaching at UCLA, I assumed that happened all the time. That wasn't the case. But one thing I was able to do consistently was display the kindness and giving attitude I learned from watching Coach Wooden. His example started in practice and carried over to game days. I know a lot of coaches that are yellers and screamers and use foul language, even toward the officials. Coach Wooden never did any of that. If he got upset with a player, he would say, "Goodness gracious sakes alive!" Those were the strongest words one would ever hear from him.

Off the court, Coach Wooden possessed that same attitude. He often talked about the importance of doing something nice for someone every day. It didn't have to be anything material. It could just be a kind word, a smile or a pat on the back. It was a way of life for him. I have tried to treat people—the managers, trainers and any others who make the basketball program function—the same way as he did. In the 40 years I've been at Louisville, I'd like to think that some of Coach Wooden's kindness rubbed off on me.

Coach Wooden knew something that many people today have forgotten: helping others and showing kindness is our responsibility as human beings. We are called to treat others with love, respect and friendship. It's something that should be a part of who we are, devoid of ulterior motives. We should be kind because we want to do so, not because we want something in return.

In Luke 6:35, Jesus says, "Love your enemies, do [what is] good, and lend, expecting nothing in return." Likewise, the apostle Paul encourages us in 2 Thessalonians 3:13 to "not grow weary in doing good." The more we practice kindness, the more it becomes a regular part of our day and who we are. We don't have to get up in the morning and say, "Hey, I'm going to be nice to people today." We'll just do it simply because that's the way it's supposed to be.

WOODEN'S WISDOM

There is always great joy in learning that something you've said or done has been meaningful to another, especially when you do it without any thought of receiving anything in return.

TRAINING TIME

1. How would your relationships with others be different if you made an effort to treat them with kindness and respect?

2. Read Luke 6:35. What is one kind thing you can do this week for someone who has wronged you?

3. How can you practice kindness and giving towards others this week?

PRAYER

Father, help me to follow Your example of kindness and giving towards others. Help me to treat everyone with kindness and respect, no matter how they treat me in return. I want to experience the joy of helping others!

Denny Crum is the former men's basketball coach at the University of Louisville and a member of the Naismith Memorial Basketball Hall of Fame. In 30 seasons, he led the Cardinals to a pair of NCAA Championships (1980 and 1986) and was named National Coach of the Year three times (1980, 1983, and 1986). He currently serves at Louisville as a special assistant to the university president.

Family Matters

BY KRISTY CURRY

Head Coach, Women's Basketball, Texas Tech University

The most important profession in the world is parenting. The second is teaching, and everyone is a teacher to someone.

JOHN WOODEN

Anyone who knows me well shouldn't be surprised that I ended up coaching women's basketball. That's because coaching truly is a family affair. It's something my grandfather, parents, brother and husband have done. Because of my family background, I was exposed to all things related to coaching.

Everyone in our family knew about Coach Wooden. As I got to know Coach personally, I learned that we shared more than just the coaching profession. We both had a strong commitment to family and a passion for teaching.

That connection was reaffirmed in 1999 when I took over the defending championship program at Purdue. In my seven years at West Lafayette, I learned that Coach Wooden had been born and raised in Indiana on a farm much like I had been raised in Olla, Louisiana. I considered it an honor to coach in the same building where he became an All-American basketball star.

During my days at Purdue, I became friends with Jane Albright, who at the time was the head women's basketball coach at Wisconsin. Jane went out of her way to welcome me to the Big 10, and we became the best of friends. I found out later that she also had a very close relationship with Coach Wooden. Through her personal stories, my respect and admiration for him steadily grew.

When people ask about my most special coaching memory, I tell them that playing in the 2001 national championship game was pretty special, but right along with that were the opportunities I had to sit down with Coach Wooden. When we traveled to Los Angeles for a game against UCLA, I took our entire coaching staff along with me to meet with Coach Wooden for the first time.

During our conversation, it was evident that he had always made his family a priority. His children, grandchildren and great-grandchildren were extremely important to him. I will always remember when he told us that he wrote a letter to his wife, Nell, every year on her birthday, their wedding anniversary and on many other special occasions, and put it under her pillow. Every single day he would think of her. Though she had been gone for 25 years, he was still as much in love with her as the day they were married.

Coach Wooden didn't let basketball define who he was as a person. That message hit home for me. Early in my coaching career, life was about nothing but basketball. My faith was (and still is) very important to me, but it wasn't until my girls started to grow up that I realized the heavy responsibility of being a parent. In many ways, Kelsey and Kendall have made me better at my job, but there's no doubt that being a good mom is much more important than being a good coach.

Many of the truths I've embraced over the years were the same ones modeled by Coach Wooden. They came from God's Word. One such principle is found in Proverbs 22:6: "Teach a youth about the way he should go; even when he is old he will not depart from it."

As a coach, I have 15 players on my team that are someone else's little girls. While they're under my care, I'm a surrogate parent to them. Coach Wooden helped me understand that fact even more. During the times I spent with him, it was evident he had incredible love for his players. He told story after story about them—stories that happened years ago, but he retold them with such vivid detail it was as if they had happened yesterday.

Some of his stories involved a difficult decision he had to make to discipline a star player by keeping him on the bench. Such was the case with his All-American guard Walt Hazzard, who would become an even better player because of Coach Wooden's loving care. He would also quote his former player Swen Nater, who wrote more than 100 poems for the beloved coach. Each of those instances exhibited the subtle but obvious passion that Coach Wooden had for those men.

If I could pinpoint a time when Coach Wooden impacted me the most, it would be the time he gave me a poem titled "A Little Fellow Follows Me" along with a written note that said, "The original of this poem was presented to me in 1936 upon the birth of my son. It has been kept nearby since then." The poem went as follows:

A careful man I want to be,
A little fellow follows me;
I do not dare to go astray,
For fear he'll go the self-same way.
I cannot once escape his eyes,
Whate'er he sees me do, he tries;
Like me he says he's going to be,
The little chap who follows me.
He thinks that I am good and fine,
Believes in every word of mine;
The base in me he must not see,
The little chap who follows me.

I must remember as I go,
Through summer's sun and winter's snow;
I'm building for the years to be
That little chap who follows me.

Coach Wooden's gift touched me as a parent. The copy he gave me is still hanging on my wall in the office. That's how special it is to me.

As a parent, somebody is always watching. Children want to be led. They want to be pushed. They want to do well. And they are watching everything we say and do. The same holds true as a leader: someone is always watching. We need to understand that and bear that great responsibility and blessing.

Coach Wooden understood that responsibility and modeled the kind of priorities that I hope to reflect in my life: putting God first, my family second, and everything else—coaching included—in its proper place.

WOODEN'S WISDOM

A coach ought to be interested in people and their welfare. Such an interest best comes from a foundation of spirituality. People in my profession have a priceless entrustment. I had to deal with young men who were under tremendous stress physically, mentally and emotionally. I had to be strong. . . . Without spiritual strength I'm not sure how good of a job I could have done. I'm certain my teaching would have suffered.

TRAINING TIME

1. Who is one person in your life that looks to you as a teacher?

2. How does putting God first in your life help you be a better parent and teacher?

3. Read 1 Timothy 4:12. How can you be a better example for your family and other believers?

PRAYER

Father, thank You for the responsibility of being a parent and a teacher. Help me to make You my first priority and be a godly example to my children and others. Help me to represent You in a way that pleases You and points others to Your love.

Kristy Curry is the head women's basketball coach at Texas Tech. She previously spent seven years at Purdue where her teams won two Big Ten regular season titles (2001, 2002) and three Big Ten Tournament championships (2000, 2003, and 2004). In her second season as a head coach, Curry guided Purdue to the NCAA championship game.

Role of a Lifetime

BY JAY CARTY

Former Assistant Coach, Men's Basketball, UCLA,
and Founder, Yes! Ministries

God made each of us unique.
JOHN WOODEN

I am one of few basketball players who never played for Coach Wooden but whom he still considered "one of his boys." His impact on my life story has been great; in fact, on two occasions Coach Wooden changed the direction of my path.

The first time was in 1962 when our Oregon State squad was soundly defeated in the Elite Eight by Coach Wooden's UCLA Bruins. I had a terrible game, and we got hammered 88-69. Two years later, I coached the freshman team at Oregon State while working on my Master's Degree. From there, I moved to Los Angeles to work on my doctorate in the School of Public Health at UCLA.

That same year, a big, tall kid from New York was entering his freshman year at UCLA. He had been recruited to play for Coach Wooden, but that was in the days when freshmen couldn't play with the varsity. This talented young athlete was going to have a wasted year.

I was bored and needed something to do, so I asked Coach Wooden if I could work out against this freshman player and create some coaching drills to help him develop. Coach agreed and put me on staff on a trial basis. Eventually, I earned a full-time spot on the coaching staff. At the same time, I'd been playing in a summer league and doing pretty well. Toward the end of the 1968-69 season, the Lakers offered me a contract, and I finished out the year playing on a team that made the NBA Finals.

Practicing every day against the 7' 2" freshman Lew Alcindor, who later became known as Kareem Abdul-Jabbar, helped me to become good enough to earn a spot with the Lakers as a 27-year-old rookie. I ultimately owe the opportunity to Coach Wooden, who took a chance on an unproven kid from Oregon State.

The second time Coach Wooden took a chance on me turned out to be substantially more significant and, rhetorically speaking, saved my life. A few years ago, I lost the use of a vocal chord. My voice start fizzling out the longer I talked. I had been an evangelist for 25 years, and suddenly I had to stop preaching. In one svelte swoop, a paralyzed vocal chord cost me my vocation, my ministry, my identity and almost everything else.

I spent about six months trying to figure out what to do. I had an idea for a children's book, and a friend of mine who went to UCLA suggested that I go talk to Coach Wooden, as he was also thinking about writing a children's book. So I went, and he greeted me as a long lost friend. I presented my idea to him, but he already had a publisher for his children's book, so it wasn't a match.

But on my way home, I got the idea for *Coach Wooden One-on-One*. I called Coach as soon as I could. Even though he already had publishers lined up for his other books, he graciously accepted my project. I know it wasn't because of what I could do for him, but he knew the fragile state of mind I was in and empathized with the challenges I was facing. Coach Wooden, in essence, ministered to me by saying yes to that book and set my life on a brand-new, exciting course.

In both of those instances, God opened the door for me to use some unique talents with which He blessed me. Back in the '60s, it was my height and my adequate basketball skill. More recently, with Coach Wooden and the publishing deal, it was an ability to communicate and minister through the written word.

Coach Wooden also helped me understand the importance of individuality. He believed that we should always "refrain from comparing ourselves to others and stay off other people's ladders of success." He believed it was more important to make the most out of our talents than to strive for achievement based on what someone else had accomplished.

As an evangelist, if I compared myself to Billy Graham, I'd get really beat up over that. I wasn't anointed to do the work that he did. It's God's job to use me to influence others in the way that He has planned. If your job is to win one particular person to Christ in the course of your lifetime and you do it, you'll get the same "well done" that Billy gets.

With that in mind, I simply need to do the best I can and let God open the doors for me. When I start getting ahead of Him and opening the doors myself, I start getting in trouble. So often, our problem is also tied to a lack of understanding regarding the individual roles within the Body of Christ. First Corinthians 12 talks about how all believers have a spiritual gift that is vital to the Church's success:

> Now there are different gifts, but the same Spirit. There are different ministries, but the same Lord. And there are different activities, but the same God is active in everyone (vv. 4-6).

In verses 8-10, Paul goes on to talk about some of those spiritual gifts, such as wisdom, faith, healing and prophecy. And in verses 12-26, he gives a beautiful analogy between the Church and the human body. I love what Paul writes in verse 14: "So the body is not one part but many."

If we grasp on to the truth of God-ordained individuality, it gives us the freedom to be who He called us to be and unshackles us from the chains of conformity. We can then take on the role of our lifetime and achieve the true biblical success that Coach Wooden and I redefined in our *One-on-One* book as a life that "places faith in the hands of the Savior."

WOODEN'S WISDOM

Each one of us has a different mix of talents and a distinctive set of circumstances. . . . If we refrain from comparing ourselves to others and stay off other people's ladders of success, we will have peace of mind. If we put forward our best effort, we can consider ourselves to be successful.

TRAINING TIME

1. Why is it easy to compare yourself to others and measure your success according to their "ladders of success"?

2. Read 1 Corinthians 12:1-27. What are some unique talents and gifts God has given you in order to serve Him?

3. How would your life be different if you grasped on to the truth of God-ordained individuality?

PRAYER

Father, thank You for giving me individuality and blessing me with spiritual gifts and unique talents. Help me to avoid comparing myself to others and focus on being who You called me to be.

Jay Carty is an award-winning author and founder of Yes! Ministries. He played basketball for Oregon State and served as an assistant coach under Coach Wooden at UCLA. Carty played one season in the NBA for the Western Division champion Los Angeles Lakers in 1968-69. He is also the co-author, with Coach Wooden, of *Coach Wooden One-on-One* and *Coach Wooden's Pyramid of Success.*

20

Legacy

JOHN MAXWELL
Author, Motivational Speaker, EQUIP

Make each day your masterpiece.
JOHN WOODEN

There was never a time when I was visiting with John Wooden that the phone didn't ring with one of his former players on the line. His influence ran long and deep—not only through his books, but also through his coaching and the relationships he had built. He breathed into men 40, 50 years younger than himself. I believe that was the essence of John Wooden: he gave more than he took.

Coach Wooden embodied a beautiful model of legacy. Our legacy is defined by what we do with the gifts that God has given to us. Coach took the gifts that God gave to him—all of those wonderful character traits that he crafted into the Pyramid of Success—and passed them on to players, family, friends and many others who have been impacted from a distance. Coach Wooden's legacy lives on in so many of us, including me.

I first met Coach Wooden on February 20, 2003, my birthday. I prepared for three days. I read everything I could find about him and wrote six pages of notes. When we finally met, I peppered him with so many questions that I felt a little embarrassed. But Coach Wooden was so kind and patient. After that time, I tried to see him once or twice a year. We usually started out with small talk, but then Coach would graciously move things forward. "John, let's get to your questions," he would say. "I know you want to get to your questions."

On one particular visit, I asked Coach Wooden how he came up with his famous quote, "Make each day your masterpiece." He told a story about watching his players in practice one day and realizing that they were not giving 100 percent. So he pulled them aside and said, "I know you're tired, and maybe you didn't do well on your exam or maybe your girlfriend broke up with you, and you're only giving me about half today. I know you're thinking that tomorrow you'll give 150 percent. But you can't give 150 percent. You can only give 100 percent. What you leave on the table today, you leave for good."

When Coach Wooden told me that story, I was already playing with the idea for a book called *Today Matters*. I remember leaving that day so energized that I thought to myself, *I have got to write this book as quickly as I can*. In that regard, Coach Wooden was both the catalyst and the motivation for *Today Matters*.

Through Coach Wooden's example, I learned that the secret of one's success is determined by his or her daily agenda. At each practice, Coach Wooden was so focused on teaching his players the right principles and values. He never asked a team to win a game for him. Winning was a byproduct of doing the right thing every day.

When you make each day a masterpiece, you are building a legacy. I learned this firsthand from Coach Wooden at an event where I brought in 80 CEOs to hear from Coach and legendary Tennessee women's basketball coach Pat Summitt. When I interviewed them, I asked Coach Wooden (then 95 years old),

"Coach, you're getting up in age. You're going to die someday. What do you want to be known for?"

Just as quickly as I'd asked the question, he looked at me, gave his distinctive shake of the head, and said, "Well, John, it certainly wouldn't be for national championships and trophies." The crowd literally gasped out loud. He continued, "If there's anything I could be known for, I'd like to be known for the fact that I was kind to people and valued them."

We were all thinking about his accomplishments, but he was teaching us that the trophies and championships were nothing but a byproduct of making every day a masterpiece.

John Wooden's legacy is bigger today than it was when he coached. I'm not just talking about the Presidential Medal of Freedom that George W. Bush gave him or the fact that the NCAA college basketball player of the year annually wins the John R. Wooden Award. All of that is nice, but he is bigger today than ever because he is humble enough to realize that making each day a masterpiece is what really produces greatness.

Legacy ought to be essential to those of us who follow Christ. We believe in eternal matters. If we didn't believe in Christ and simply believed death was the end, we would probably live only to please ourselves. But we have a greater plan and understand the truth found in Ephesians 5:15-16: "Pay careful attention, then, to how you walk—not as unwise people but as wise—making the most of the time, because the days are evil."

Most of us will never leave a legacy as immense as Coach Wooden's, but each of us can leave a legacy with eternal impact. When we choose to give 100 percent of ourselves each day, it is possible to leave a worthy heritage to our family, friends and those people who daily intersect with our lives.

Why not start leaving a great legacy now? Make today a masterpiece.

WOODEN'S WISDOM

Don't measure yourself by what you have accomplished,
but by what you should have accomplished with your ability.
You can't live a perfect day without doing something for someone
who will never be able to repay you.

TRAINING TIME

1. As Christians, why should we be concerned about legacy?

2. What are some steps you can take to make each day a master-piece?

3. Answer the question that John Maxwell asked Coach Wooden: "You're going to die someday. What do you want to be known for?"

PRAYER

Father, I want to leave a positive legacy to my family, friends
and those around me. Help me to live out the character traits
needed to make each day a masterpiece. Help me to reflect
Your integrity, Your spirit, and Your heart.

John C. Maxwell is an internationally respected leadership expert, speaker and author who has sold more than 18 million books. Dr. Maxwell is the founder of EQUIP, a non-profit organization that has trained more than 5 million leaders in 126 countries worldwide. Each year he speaks to the leaders of diverse organizations, such as Fortune 500 companies, foreign governments, the National Football League, the United States Military Academy at West Point, and the United Nations. A *New York Times*, *Wall Street Journal*, and *Business Week* best-selling author, Maxwell has written three books that have sold more than a million copies: *The 21 Irrefutable Laws of Leadership*, *Developing the Leader Within You*, and *The 21 Indispensable Qualities of a Leader*. His blog can be read at JohnMaxwellOnLeadership.com.

21

Shaping Up

BY DOUG MCINTOSH
Former NCAA Center, UCLA

As a basketball player, I wanted to be in the best possible physical condition.
JOHN WOODEN

When I was a senior in high school, I thought I knew everything about playing basketball. But when I arrived on the UCLA campus as a freshman the fall of 1962, little did I know that I was going to receive quite an education from John Wooden.

Coach Wooden's attention to detail impacted all of his players. We learned something new that very first day of practice, in fact, when he showed us how to properly put on our socks and shoes. Coach Wooden insisted that shoes fit well and shoelaces be snug at the bottom as well as at the top.

Making sure we had the basics right was linked to Coach Wooden's firm belief that his players should always be in the best physical condition possible. During my sophomore season, we had a dramatic illustration of this philosophy. After assessing our team's particular skills and talents, Coach Wooden concluded that we should implement a 2-2-1 zone press. He knew that we didn't have a lot of size (our tallest starter was 6' 5"), but we did possess above-average quickness.

Our practices started October 15, and we didn't get a taste of the zone press until around Thanksgiving, about two weeks before the season started. By then, we were in good shape. I personally thought that I was in top form. And then we started practicing the press. I discovered quickly that I wasn't in any kind of condition at all. It was like starting all over again.

But once we finally began to use the zone press in games, we became used to the intensity of the play. Our opponents would handle it just fine for a while and then about the middle of the first half, the fatigue level would kick in and they would start making mistakes. By then, you could see the exhaustion in their faces. That's when we knew we had them.

Conditioning was the heart and soul of that team, and probably the primary reason we were able to go undefeated and win the national championship. I always tell people that the toughest opponents we faced that year were our second string. They were seldom intimidated by it, and they were in the kind of shape the starters were. With other opponents, however, we enjoyed a psychological advantage because of the extraordinary conditioning we experienced.

I've taken the lessons I learned from Coach Wooden about conditioning and found ways to apply them to all areas of my life. This is especially true when I've found myself facing challenges. Because Coach Wooden pushed us so hard, it's now easy for me to remember that I can always dig a little deeper and find some strength in me that I didn't know I had.

Conditioning also applies to our spiritual lives. Spiritual growth and discipleship are very much like becoming a good athlete. In 1 Corinthians 9:25-27, the apostle Paul uses an athletic illustration to make this very point:

> Now everyone who competes exercises self-control in everything. However, they do it to receive a perishable

crown, but we an imperishable one. Therefore I do not run like one who runs aimlessly, or box like one who beats the air. Instead, I discipline my body and bring it under strict control, so that after preaching to others, I myself will not be disqualified.

It requires consistent spiritual conditioning to become a disciplined follower of Christ. You have to apply yourself every day. You cannot neglect the inner life for weeks at a time and expect that everything will fall into place in a healthy and blessed way. You have to get with God and get the Bible out and meditate on the Scriptures. Otherwise, you'll find yourself sliding into bad habits and becoming vulnerable to temptations and all kinds of problems.

Coach Wooden aimed at getting us in the best condition possible, but not just to win a championship. He knew that such conditioning would help us later in life. Certainly he was a competitive man, but Coach Wooden always had the right motivation. First and foremost, he wanted to help his teams develop into great men, not just great players.

It's a hard lesson to learn and I don't know that I've always reflected it, but I've discovered that it doesn't matter if you work for a gold medal, play for an NCAA championship or pastor a church, you honor God by exerting yourself to the maximum and exercising self-control in all things.

As Paul writes in Colossians 3:23, "Whatever you do, do it enthusiastically, as something done for the Lord and not for men." It's true in business. It's true in scholarship. It's true in athletics. It's true in ministry. It's true across the board. You are accountable to God for the gifts that He's given you. You can't answer to other people's expectations. Just as Coach Wooden has done throughout his life, you simply have to honor God by giving Him the best you have.

WOODEN'S WISDOM

*There was a time when I'd tell myself, "I'm going to be in better
condition than anyone else." As I grew older, my thinking changed to,
"I'm going to be in the best possible condition I can be."
I had learned that I only have control over myself.*

TRAINING TIME

1. Read 1 Corinthians 9:25-27. Why is it important to condition
   yourself spiritually?

2. What are some practical steps you can apply daily to condition yourself spiritually?

3. When it comes to spiritual conditioning, do you have the
   right motivation?

PRAYER

*Father, I want to honor You by giving You the best that I have.
Examine my heart and expose any wrong motivations
within me. Help me to have the discipline to condition
myself spiritually every day.*

Doug McIntosh is the senior pastor and co-founder of Cornerstone Bible Church in Lilburn, Georgia. He is a published author and serves as a member of the Board of Directors of Wycliffe Bible Translators USA. McIntosh was a starter on UCLA's 1965 national championship team.

22

The Real You

BY JOHN NABER

Olympic Champion, Swimming

---

*Most people think of poise as calm, self-assured dignity;
but I call it "just being you."*

JOHN WOODEN

"Nice to meet you, John," Coach Wooden said to me as I introduced myself at a Character Counts seminar in Arizona. Coach was a special guest and had just been interviewed by Bob Costas in front of a live, adoring audience.

Now that might not seem like a big thing, but there were two things about that simple greeting that immediately struck me.

First of all, he referred to me as John, despite the fact that so many people get confused and call me "Jim," due to my name's similarity to Jim Nabor, the actor who played Gomer Pyle on the *Andy Griffith Show*.

But what really impacted me was the way he said hello. It was in the congenial tones of someone who already knew me well. I quickly realized why he was so revered. From that moment, I felt a real connection to this man who exuded great poise and in turn gave me the courage to do the same.

When John Wooden modeled poise, he was, in a way, telling me that I too could be myself. I should be comfortable in my own skin. His example allowed me to be more genuine, which is, frankly, a great blessing when I'm standing in front of a camera or speaking to a huge audience. Poise allows me to enjoy the experience and be the best me that I can be, as opposed to trying to be a very good somebody else.

As an Olympian, I've found this concept of poise to be paramount in how athletes deal with intense pressure. For most of them, the Olympics are a once-in-a-lifetime experience. It's frightening when you just get one shot, and your performance will determine how the world will measure you the rest of your life. It's very easy to lose your composure.

Snowboard cross-athlete Seth Wescott showed great poise during the 2010 Olympics. In his sport, four snowboarders race down an obstacle course at the same time. There is a lot of bumping, and racers often go off course and crash. Seth realized right away that the jumps were placed closer together than his speed would allow. He had a decision to make. He could back off and play it safe, or he could land beyond the bump and lose some of the momentum he had going into the next jump.

Seth chose to be his natural self and let the race take care of itself. Sure enough, he was in last place just five seconds into the race, but he gradually picked away at the other competitors. When the straightaway came, he had plenty of natural speed to go past his opposition and win the first U.S. gold in Vancouver. That took a great deal of poise and confidence in his ability.

I've found the same to be true in my broadcasting career. When I'm staring at a television camera and the little red tally light goes on to indicate that we're live on the air, I can't worry about what the people watching are going to think about me.

Instead, I need to concentrate on being the best me that I can be. I don't want to accept weaknesses or mistakes and say, "Oh well, that's just the way I was made." But I do need to remember that what I'm doing isn't to, as Coach Wooden says, "live up to others' expectations."

That doesn't mean we should live to satisfy our own expectations. We should, however, live according to what we think God would want of us. In other words, it's perfectly okay to try to live up to God's expectations. That's because God genuinely knows who we are and of what we are capable. Psalm 139:1 says, "LORD, You have searched me and known me."

God doesn't want us to be anything but who He created us to be. His expectations of us are accurate. Life is more peaceful and fulfilling when we seek to live up to God's expectations. Romans 12:1-2 gives us one way that we can do that:

> Therefore, brothers, by the mercies of God, I urge you to present your bodies as a living sacrifice, holy and pleasing to God; this is your spiritual worship. Do not be conformed to this age, but be transformed by the renewing of your mind, so that you may discern what is the good, pleasing, and perfect will of God.

When we try to conform to someone else's expectations, we're taking two big gambles. First of all, we may have misinterpreted their expectations altogether. Second, we may be trying to do something that goes against the very DNA that God gave us.

That's the beauty of Coach Wooden's definition of poise. It gives us the freedom to be ourselves and operate within the confines of God's plans for our lives, which Jeremiah 29:11 says are "to give you a future and a hope."

WOODEN'S WISDOM

When we have poise, we're not acting, faking or pretending. We're not trying to be something we're not, nor are we attempting to live up to others' expectations. Therefore, when we are being who we really are, we'll have a greater likelihood of functioning nearer our own level of competency.

TRAINING TIME

1. Has there ever been a time when you tried to be someone else instead of who God made you to be?

2. Read Psalm 139. How does this Scripture passage change your view of yourself?

3. Read Romans 12:1-2. According to these verses, how do you avoid the pitfall of conforming to other people's expectations instead of God's?

PRAYER

Father, thank You for making me just the way I am. I don't want to spend my time trying to please other people and live up to their expectations. Help me to live up to Your expectations by being the best me I can be.

John Naber is a retired American swimmer with four gold medals and one silver medal from the 1976 Olympic Games in Montreal. He has covered sports events for ABC, CBS, NBC, FOX, ESPN and Turner Broadcasting. Naber is the author of *Awaken the Olympian Within* and *Eureka: How Innovation Changes the Olympic Games (and Everything Else)*. He currently works as a motivational speaker and corporate trainer.

23

Prayer Works

BY NAPOLEON KAUFMAN
Former NFL Running Back, Oakland Raiders

When counseling my players who had problems off the court,
I always recommended prayer.

JOHN WOODEN

People tend to get a little uncomfortable when athletes and coaches start talking about prayer. Believers and non-believers alike sometimes question the role this spiritual practice has within the world of sports. Sometimes it's an overzealous approach to evangelism that serves as the culprit to the public's wary response.

Statements like, "God helped us win the game," or "Jesus gave me the strength to score that touchdown" have caused a great deal of discomfort and have sometimes fostered a malcontent attitude towards prayer and the Christian faith in general.

To this former NFL athlete who now serves as a senior pastor, that's what makes Coach Wooden's approach to prayer so appealing. In his book *Coach Wooden One-on-One*, he writes, "I never encouraged anyone to pray for a win." He wanted his players to "honor God by doing their best, controlling their emotions, and asking for protection."

When it came to off-the-court matters, Coach Wooden en-couraged his players to pray when they faced difficult times and tough decisions. That's because Coach Wooden himself was a man of prayer and recognized its significance.

Coach Wooden understood that "God hears all of our prayers." That statement rings true in several ways. For the sinner who has no relationship with God, 1 John 1:9 tells us that "if we confess our sins, He is faithful and righteous to forgive us our sins and to cleanse us from all unrighteousness." For the believer who has a relationship with God, Proverbs 15:29 confirms that "He hears the prayer of the righteous."

God is omniscient. He knows everything. And it pleases Him when people realize that He is their source of strength and has the ability to answer prayers. Coach Wooden believed that God answers prayers. This truth is illustrated in Luke 11:9, where Jesus says, "Keep asking, and it will be given to you. Keep searching, and you will find. Keep knocking, and the door will be opened to you." It might be instantaneous or take a while, but according to the Word, answers will be found through faithful prayer.

When answers come, they may not always be what we want. As Coach Wooden says, "Sometimes the answer is no." The key to this difficult truth is found in 1 John 5:14-15: "Now this is the confi-dence we have before Him; whenever we ask anything according to His will, He hears us. And if we know that He hears whatever we ask, we know that we have what we have asked Him for."

Even our Savior experienced this harsh reality when He was on His way to the cross. As He prayed in the garden, Jesus was feeling pain and anguish. In that moment, Matthew 26:39 says He prayed, "My Father! If it is possible, let this cup pass from Me." But then He submitted to God and declared, "Yet not as I will, but as You will."

That is the key to walking with God. Sometimes He tells us no because there's a greater purpose. For Jesus, it meant going through the most difficult thing imaginable that ultimately made the gift of salvation and eternal life possible, even though at that moment it wasn't something He, in His flesh, wanted to do. Jesus prayed for relief, but God said no.

Ultimately, it's not about our will. It's about His will. Sometimes God says no to keep us from things He knows can potentially harm us. I'm glad God has said no to me. There have been many occasions where I've prayed for things I wanted. God said no, but then gave me what I needed. That's the beauty of prayer. It's about His will being done—not mine.

This was especially true in my life when I was contemplating retiring from the NFL and entering full-time ministry. I was only 27 years old and arguably had more productive days left in me. It was a trying time. I was in the midst of a storm, and people were saying I'd lost my mind and called me foolish for considering it.

There was a time when I wondered if I was making the right decision. Was it really what God wanted me to do? If I had not maintained an active prayer life and taken the time to seek God's face in prayer, I don't think I could have made the decision. But the more I prayed, the more God confirmed in my heart what I was supposed to do.

The key isn't just asking for direction; it's about being responsive to His play and being willing to walk through the door He has opened. As it says in Luke 11:9, many times God is knocking, but we're not available. When we make ourselves available, we can count on the fact that God is always there. If He has anything to say, it's up to us to position ourselves to listen.

Most people who have met Coach Wooden talk about how much he loved building relationships with others. Even with his players, over time he went from being their coach to being their friend. That's what Christianity is about. It's about life and having a living, breathing relationship with God.

For me, praying isn't just a matter of doing what you're supposed to do. It's a matter of loving God and wanting to talk to

Him. I want to talk to Him before I go to bed and when I get up in the morning. I want to talk to Him when I'm walking down the street or driving my car. It has to become life. That's what prayer has become for me, for Coach Wooden, and for those who pursue a relationship with the Creator.

WOODEN'S WISDOM

I always told [my players] I was sure God hears all of our prayers and answers them—but sometimes the answer is no.

TRAINING TIME

1. Has there been a time in your life when you prayed and God told you no?

2. How has God given you direction in difficult circumstances through prayer?

3. Read Luke 11:19. What is a current situation in your life that requires you to consistently seek God's guidance through prayer?

PRAYER

Father, thank You for the gift of communicating with You through prayer. Give me courage to trust You when You answer, even when the answer is no. Help me to listen and be responsive when You speak to me.

Napoleon Kaufman is a retired running back who spent six years in the NFL playing for the Oakland Raiders. At the University of Washington, he was a second-team All-American and still holds the school record for career rushing yards (4,106) and career rushing touchdowns (34). Kaufman currently serves as senior pastor at The Well Christian Community Church in Dublin, California.

24

Friends Are Friends

BY JANE ALBRIGHT
Head Coach, Women's Basketball, University of Nevada at Reno

Friends help each other; they don't use each other.
JOHN WOODEN

When you've been friends with someone long enough, you're sure to have your fair share of funny stories. My friendship with Coach Wooden goes back 25 years, but one of our more comical moments happened about 17 years earlier when I first met him at a Medalist basketball clinic in Myrtle Beach, South Carolina.

At that time, I was a first-year high school coach. I graduated from Appalachian State in 1977, where my assistant coach introduced me to Coach Wooden's book *They Call Me Coach*. My senior year, I even wore Coach Wooden's Bata brand custom polyurethane shoes. The only problem was that they had virtually no traction, and when I ran in them, I slid clumsily all over the court.

When I went to the clinic, I was very excited about my opportunity to learn from Coach Wooden. I even skipped being in my cousin's wedding to be there. At that time, Coach Wooden was just three years removed from his final season and national championship at UCLA. He was easily the authority on college basketball. When given the chance to meet Coach and ask him a question, all I could do was talk about those shoes.

"How can I keep from sliding all over the floor in your Bata shoes?" I asked.

Why would you tell someone whose name was on the shoe that they weren't very good? But that's what I did. Coach Wooden graciously advised me to scratch the soles with steel wool to get better traction. I still laugh thinking about what an idiot I was. Coach and I also had a good chuckle reliving that story, because that's what friends do.

By the time I was coaching at Wisconsin in 1994, I considered myself a Coach Wooden groupie. I was given the opportunity to travel to Los Angeles with Florida State head coach Sue Semrau, one of my assistants then, and meet with him. Cori Close set up the meeting and joined us. Cori is now at Florida State with Sue, but at the time was serving as an assistant at UCLA. That first introduction opened the door to what I now consider one of my dearest friendships.

At first I was overwhelmed by the thought of sitting and talking with Coach Wooden. But over time, I began to get more comfortable and glean much more from the relationship. As a Christian, I had a principled understanding of true friendship. But in Coach Wooden, I saw it modeled in a way I'd never seen before. He was the most like Jesus of any person I'd ever met. I think it was because of the love, honor and friendship that he gave to people like me who had nothing to give him in return.

Coach Wooden's example of friendship changed my outlook on coaching. Clear boundaries are needed with players, but it's obvious that his players were extremely important to him. He has fostered long-term relationships with his players, and he talked about those relationships with such sincerity.

But it wasn't just the stories about his former players that inspired me. On several occasions while visiting Coach Wooden, I had the opportunity to see him interact with former players. During one memorable meal at VIPs, All-American Michael Warren from UCLA's 1967 and 1968 championship teams dropped in unannounced. I clumsily referred to him as "Bobby" because of his famous television role on the 1980s police drama *Hill Street Blues*. But even in my awestruck state, I could recognize the unique bond that Coach Wooden maintained with him as well as so many of the other young men he impacted at UCLA.

My friendship with Coach Wooden strengthened me, and now I model this type of friendship to my teams. My former players visit all the time and stay at my house. I'll bring them to meet my team and tell the players, "I've known this person longer than you've been alive." And they laugh. I challenge my players in their friendships. I ask them when last talked to their high school coach. I encourage them to reconnect with their best friend from second grade. It's important that they understand the value of friendship and put the time and effort into life-affirming connections. I teach them that maintaining friendship requires key characteristics such as patience, forgiveness, and unconditional love.

Coach Wooden modeled patience to me in our personal interactions and when I brought my teams to meet him. I remember one particular instance when I brought my 2008-2009 Nevada team to his condo during a road trip. That particular day we visited with Coach for almost five hours. We knew we needed to leave, but he talked to every player on my team, took individual pictures, and signed autographs. He asked each of them about themselves. It was amazing.

At the end of the night as I was hugging him goodbye, I said, "Coach, thank you for spending so much time with my team." He looked at me, smiled and said, "Jane, that's why patience is at the top of my Pyramid."

Friendship also requires forgiveness. I remember the first time I visited Coach Wooden and asked, "How will I know if I'm a good coach?" He said, "Jane, you won't know for 20 years." That's friendship—a long-term relationship. Most people today only have expendable relationships. People take you off their Facebook friends list if they get mad at you. When you're friends with someone for 25 years, the relationship only lasts because of grace and forgiveness.

Jesus talks a lot about forgiveness. It's not a natural thing to do. It's hard to forgive someone when they've hurt you. Jesus made that point with Peter in Matthew 18:22. He explained that he was required to forgive a brother "not as many as seven . . . but 70 times seven." He wasn't literally telling Peter to forgive his transgressor 490 times, but was symbolically explaining that forgiveness is a forever kind of action. Forgiveness also speaks to another trait friendship needs to survive—unconditional love.

Unconditional love is what keeps friendship together in the first place. And it opens the door for others to see the nature of God through our lives. That's why in John 13:35, Jesus says, "By this all people will know that you are My disciples, if you have love for one another."

That's the kind of love that I hope I modeled in my friendship with Coach Wooden. Sometimes I didn't feel like I had anything to give him, yet our relationship was based on, as he would say, "mutual esteem and devotion" for each other. And most importantly, we had our faith in Christ as the common bond.

WOODEN'S WISDOM

If we are going to successfully work with others, it is vital to know the role of friendship. Friendship comes from mutual esteem and devotion. Friendship is doing for others while they are doing for you. It's called ministry when all of the doing goes in one direction. Friendship goes both ways. Friendship is like a good marriage—it's based on mutual concern.

TRAINING TIME

1. Who has modeled true, Christian friendship in your life?

2. Who is one person God may be prompting you to reconnect with and model true friendship to?

3. Read Matthew 18:21-22. Who do you need to forgive and model true friendship and Christian love toward?

PRAYER

Father, thank You for the gift of friendship.
Help me to model true friendship in all of my relationships.
Show me who needs a true friend and use me to show Your
patience, forgiveness and love to them.

Jane Albright is the head women's basketball coach at the University of Nevada at Reno. In 25 years at the collegiate level, she has amassed over 400 career wins. While the head coach at Wisconsin, she led her team to the 2000 WNIT Championship and has taken her teams to a combined nine NCAA Tournament appearances. She is the all-time winningest coach at both Wisconsin and Northern Illinois.

Competitive Paradox

BY MIKE DUNLAP

Assistant Coach, Men's Basketball, St. John's University

With competitive greatness, we can deliver our best when our best is needed; at the same time, we can make those around us better, too.

JOHN WOODEN

Here is one of sport's greatest paradoxes: How do you get a group of individuals to operate as a team? Most people, by nature, desire to fulfill their own personal agenda. Even if the motivation is pure, the fact remains that individuality and unity usually stand diametrically opposed to each other.

Coach Wooden knew how to undo that paradox. He was a highly intelligent man who understood the pragmatics of life and what motivated people. He studied the individual to see what his most selfish desire was and then used it to build a bridge to the team. For instance, he knew that the guy who sets the screen is the most selfish individual on the floor because he's going to get open.

Coach Wooden was able to get a player to take the focus off himself and motivate him to give in to the greater good of the team. He could take any group of players and get them to reach a high level of competitive greatness. He had an uncanny ability to get players to do the ordinary and really relish it.

It was these basic principles from Coach Wooden that I have taken to every coaching station in my life. I was privileged to first encounter Coach Wooden in 1971 at an awards ceremony in my hometown of Fairbanks, Alaska, when I was just 13 years old. His one-hour speech captured my attention and my imagination. A year later, I attended his basketball camp at Pepperdine University. Then, early in my career at Cal-Lutheran, I enjoyed the opportunity to know him on a more personal level. When you're with Coach Wooden one on one, you realize how smart and principled he is.

I remember being in his apartment when he explained the five laws of learning. He had an analogy for each one. I can repeat it verbatim because of the way he indelibly marked each teaching point with a story. That's what was remarkable about him. He was knowledgeable and, in his inimitable way, made sure others understood what he was trying to get across.

But the greatest lesson I took from Coach Wooden had to do with his ability to bring people together for the benefit of the team. He talked so much about effort. When you focus on the effort, then the result becomes invisible. His measure of effort led to process over result. The more you focused on the task, the less chance the result became an obstruction to achieving your goals. It's almost a contradiction, but somehow he made sense of contradiction.

I carried that concept of effort over result to my work at Metro State where our teams had an amazing nine-year run that resulted in two NCAA Division II championships. Coach Wooden taught me how to challenge the individual and show people the way to the team. I can honestly say that none of my teams missed out on competitive greatness, and I owe much to Coach Wooden.

The 2002 national championship team in particular exhibited this characteristic. That team didn't have the greatest talent, but they exceeded all expectations. That's another byproduct of giving your best. Sometimes, it results in some spectacular outcomes. Coach Wooden experienced that 10 times over, but he'd still tell you that the road to competitive greatness was just as enjoyable as the final destination.

WOODEN'S WISDOM

*A person with (competitive greatness) loves a challenge—
the tougher the better.*

TRAINING TIME

1. Are there areas in your life where you are working towards your personal agenda instead of the interests of others?

2. How can you personally benefit from giving in to the greater good of the team?

3. Read Ephesians 4:1-16. According to this Scripture, what are the benefits of Christians working together and living in unity with another?

PRAYER

*Father, thank You for placing me around people that can
push me to be better in my daily life and in my walk with You.
Help me to lay aside my personal agenda for the greater
good of the team, so we can become better individuals and
live in unity with one another.*

Mike Dunlap is an assistant basketball coach at St. John's University. As a head coach, he made his mark at Metro State College in Denver, Colorado, where he led the Roadrunners to a pair of NCAA Division II national championships (2000 and 2002). Dunlap has also served as an assistant coach with the University of Arizona, the University of Oregon and the NBA's Denver Nuggets.

Outside the Box

BY JOSH DAVIS
Olympic Champion, Swimming

---

*Resourcefulness is using our wits, proper judgment and common
sense to solve problems and meet challenges.*

JOHN WOODEN

Coach Wooden didn't necessarily seem like a creative, outside-of-the-box guy. He was a straight-laced, by-the-book kind of person. But he was always dreaming up new drills, new plays and solutions to the challenges that each new season presented. Coach Wooden taught me that it often takes unorthodox thinking to fulfill great dreams.

Coach Wooden's resourcefulness was famously displayed in his 1964 team, which used the full-court press he implemented to overcome its lack of size. That unit was the model of teamwork as it went 30-0 and upset a much taller Duke squad in the national championship. Resourcefulness was a huge key in Coach Wooden's first title.

Coach Wooden has been inspiring me to be more resourceful ever since I first heard him speak to our U.S. Swim Team in September 2000. We were preparing for the Sydney

Games later that month, and I was amazed as I listened to this 90-year-old man share all 25 points of his Pyramid of Success for 60 minutes and then answer our questions. His principles from the Pyramid enhanced my ability to be resourceful and challenged me to use those practical yet powerful tools to my advantage.

Most of my athletic career has been spent "inventing, creating, imagining, synthesizing, evaluating, classifying, observing and analyzing" ways to get the most out of the gifts and talents that God has placed within me. When I was 14, I would watch swimming videos from start to finish and read every technique book and magazine from cover to cover.

As I entered the competitive arena, I started to try things the others guys weren't willing to do or didn't know how to do. When I was 20 years old, for example, I decided to start stretching, because I had read how stretching after practice can reduce recovery time and prevent injuries. Then, when I was 23, I started studying nutrition. I radically changed my eating habits and saw a significant improvement in my health and stamina.

My out-of-the-box thinking didn't stop there. My faith in God has led me to pursue spiritual solutions to physical, emotional and mental challenges. If I had trouble sleeping before a meet, I would get out my old Walkman and listen to the Bible on tape and sermons from my favorite preachers. That routine renewed my mind and comforted my soul. And, honestly, it helped me to sleep better as well. After some meditation and prayer, I could go right to sleep with the peace of knowing that God would be with me during my race the next day. No one else on the U.S. Swim Team was doing it, but it sure worked for me.

While Coach Wooden has served as a modern-day example of resourcefulness, I've also learned from the great Bible hero

Nehemiah. He was a Jewish man who lived in the time that Judah was under Persian rule. When he got word that Jerusalem's walls had been severely breached due to the occupation, Nehemiah was saddened and desired to go back home and repair the damage. He spent days fasting and praying and asking God for favor with King Artaxerxes I, for whom he was a chief official and cupbearer.

The king granted him leave and he even received letters to ensure safe passage and timber from the king's forest to help with the rebuilding process. When Nehemiah arrived in Jerusalem, he secretly surveyed the damage and created a plan of action. His resourcefulness was most evident in the creation of a strategy to protect against the armies that opposed his efforts.

Nehemiah was very strategic in his approach. As Coach Wooden would say, he used his "wits, proper judgment and common sense" to get the job done. When the process was threatened, Nehemiah writes that, "Half of my men did the work while the other half held spears, bows, and armor" (4:16) and "The laborers who carried the loads worked with one hand and held a weapon with the other" (v. 17). Nehemiah was even resourceful in practical matters such as physical hygiene: "My brothers, my men, and the guards with me never took off our clothes. Each carried his weapon, even when washing" (v. 23).

That's the genius of resourcefulness. It's all about simplifying complex situations and transferring the solution to a problem in such a way that everyone understands and can effectively apply to the purpose of completing a task.

Nehemiah rebuilt the wall in 52 days. Coach Wooden won 10 championships in 12 years. I won 5 medals in 2 Olympics and continue to rely on resourcefulness as a motivational speaker and swimming clinician. The goals may be different, but the path to reaching them always requires creative thinking that ejects you from the box.

WOODEN'S WISDOM

[Resourcefulness] is using initiative in difficult situations and involves inventing, creating, imagining, synthesizing, evaluating, classifying, observing and analyzing solutions to overcome the trials that life throws at us. Resourcefulness is dreaming up ways to meet our goals.

TRAINING TIME

1. Has there been a time in your life when you needed to be resourceful to accomplish your goals?

2. In which areas of your life do you need to invite Jesus to be a part?

3. How can strengthening your relationship with Christ help you be more resourceful in practical matters?

PRAYER

Father, thank You for giving me the strength and creativity needed to be resourceful to accomplish Your goals for me. Help me turn to You for solutions to life's difficult situations.

Josh Davis is a two-time Olympic swimmer who won three gold medals at the 1996 Summer Games in Atlanta and two silver medals at the 2000 Summer Games in Sydney. He currently travels as a motivational speaker and runs USA Swim Clinics in an effort to teach and develop aspiring young swimmers. Josh is also the compiler and general editor of *The Goal and the Glory*.

Change of Plans

BY MIKE JARVIS

Head Coach, Men's Basketball, Florida Atlantic University

Adaptability is being able to adjust to any situation at any given time.
JOHN WOODEN

There is one thing that I've learned over a lifetime of playing and coaching: change will come, and you'd better be prepared to adapt. I've traveled down some pretty long and winding roads, and I'm thankful I had great mentors like Dick Dukeshire, my basketball coach at Northeastern University, and Red Auerbach, the legendary Boston Celtics coach and general manager, to teach me how to deal with adversity and change.

Coach Wooden also influenced me with his unshakeable character and his unwavering faith in God. At first I was drawn to him as a basketball coach. I went to Los Angeles for my first Final Four in 1968. I watched Coach Wooden on the sideline and thought to myself, *You know, someday I would love to be a big-time college coach and have a chance to coach in the NCAA Tournament.*

After coming back home, I decided to make a conscious effort to learn more about him. I started to do some homework and read about his Pyramid of Success, and I was impressed by his teaching. But it was Coach Wooden's character and core values that really captured me. He was a man of integrity who didn't compromise after reaching a high level of success. He showed incredible strength that came from his relationship with God.

That first Final Four I attended in 1968, for instance, was a great example of Coach Wooden's stellar character. UCLA defeated North Carolina handily in the championship game, but his players showed amazing poise and self-control while the team's fans engaged in hysterical celebration. Later I learned that Coach Wooden made it a point to remind his players to conduct themselves with discipline and humility, no matter the outcome.

My personal faith would come a few years later, but God provided many opportunities in my coaching career to learn about Coach Wooden's principle of adaptability, which stems from character. My first lesson came in 1977 when I was an assistant coach at Harvard. Tom "Satch" Sanders was the head coach, although he was more famous for playing on eight of Boston's NBA championship teams.

When Coach Sanders stepped down from his post, I was sure that I was going to take his place. I was going to get my first head coaching opportunity at Harvard. I remember vividly the day I was told that wouldn't be the case. When I didn't get the job, I went home that night, laid on my bed and cried like a baby. My wife, Connie, came in and grabbed me. "Listen, don't forget one thing," she said. "God loves you and He has something better in store for you."

The following year, I took the head coaching job at Cambridge Rindge and Latin High School, my alma mater. My goal after graduating college in '68 was to coach there, but instead I ended up as an assistant at Northeastern University for five years followed by a four-year stint at Harvard. I didn't realize it then, but during that time God was training me and preparing me, and, in His own way, teaching me to be patient.

When I ended up at Cambridge Rindge and Latin, I had the opportunity to coach the number one team in the country and

Patrick Ewing, the number one prep player in the country and future NBA Hall of Fame inductee. Because of our success, my career took off to a much greater extent than it likely would have if I'd been hired at Harvard.

Several years later, I ended up at St. John's University after enjoyable runs at Boston University and George Washington University. Things seemed to be going well. We won the 2003 National Invitational Tournament, I co-authored the book *Skills For Life*, and in 2004 I appeared in the movie *The Perfect Score*.

Then, just six games into the 2003-04 season, everything came crashing down. Contract negotiations stalled and then our program was riddled with off-the-court problems. Subsequently St. John's placed itself on probation. After a disappointing 2-4 start, I was fired. Suddenly I was back to square one, and I didn't know if I'd ever coach again. My wife said, "Let's get out of this crazy New York," and I agreed. She suggested we move to Florida. It was the last place I thought we would ever move. As far as I was concerned, Florida was nothing but heat and gators. But we packed up and headed south anyway.

As the LORD would have it, we found a church just five minutes from our house in Boca Raton. Pastor David Nicholas met me at the door of Spanish River Church after that first service and invited me to his men's Bible study. One year later, on April 29, 2005, I accepted Christ. Three years later, thanks to the lobbying efforts of my fellow church members, I was named head coach at Florida Atlantic. I'm convinced that God brought us to Boca Raton so my wife and I could be united together in His family. Sure, he wanted me to get back into coaching, but the plan was much grander. It took a willingness to adapt and follow the long and winding road that God had paved for me.

Coach Wooden went through similar changes in his career. While at Indiana, he wanted to take the job at Minnesota, but a snowstorm delayed their offer and he ended up at UCLA instead.

As a Midwesterner, he adapted to life on the West Coast and proceeded to build a legacy that will be felt long after his passing.

While I never expect to come close to his basketball achievements, I do hope to mirror Coach Wooden's adaptability as a coach, father, husband and, most importantly, as a follower of Christ. That's because I've learned that change is certainly going to come—one way or another.

WOODEN'S WISDOM
If we want to succeed, we must readily adapt to circumstances as they unfold—this includes both what we cannot change and what will take some time to change.

TRAINING TIME
1. In the past, how well have you adapted to change?

2. How has God used that time of change to train and prepare you for something greater?

3. How does Coach Wooden's definition of adaptability help you follow God's path for your life?

PRAYER
Father, thank You that You are in control of my life and walk with me through the long and winding road. Help me to be adaptable to Your plan and trust You through the changes.

Mike Jarvis is the men's basketball coach at Florida Atlantic University. He previously coached at Boston University, George Washington University, and St. John's University, where he took his teams to a combined nine NCAA Tournaments. Jarvis led St. John's to the 2000 Big East regular season title, and in 1990 he was named America East Coach of the Year. Coach Jarvis is the only coach to win 100 games at three different universities and 100 games at the high school level.

The Value of Inclusion

BY ERNIE JOHNSON
NBA Studio Host, TNT and NBA Network

It is easier to reach our potential when we learn the value of including others in our quest.
JOHN WOODEN

No matter how great Lew Alcindor and Bill Walton were, there's no way that one guy beats five. It's not to say Coach Wooden didn't have his share of players who thought they could take charge of a game. On the 1964 championship team, he dealt with Gail Goodrich's and Walt Hazzard's confident personalities—each one thought they should be the central figure in the offense. But in his masterful way, Coach Wooden was able to use his unique brand of psychology to help both players understand their roles and how to work together for the greater good of the team.

Coach Wooden has always been an inspiration to me, and not just from the success he had on the basketball court, but by the firm grasp he had on the qualities that transcend basketball and breed success in all areas of life. His words that reach out and grab me are those that encourage us to "learn the value of including others in our quest."

Coach Wooden's challenge reminds me of a story. There was once a basketball coach, who, like Coach Wooden, hailed from Indiana. His name was Phil Bollier and he coached high school ball in the Hoosier state. One day he picked up stakes and moved his family south to the Atlanta area, where a brand-new high school was about to open its doors for the first time.

During the first week of school, Coach Bollier was walking the halls when a sound caught his attention. It was the hum of a power wheelchair as it turned a corner and disappeared into a special needs classroom. Phil poked his head into that classroom and met the wheelchair's 16-year-old driver, Michael.

Michael, who had been adopted from Romania, had muscular dystrophy along with some developmental delays, and struggled to speak in complete sentences. When you have muscular dystrophy, your muscles get weaker as you grow older. Nothing is simple. Coach Bollier picked up on the fact that one of his favorite things to say was, "Love you, too," even if you hadn't said it to him first. Their short exchange that day would prove to be life-altering.

Coach Bollier sent a note home from school asking Michael's parents if it would be okay for their son to be part of the high school basketball program. He described Michael as a five-foot tall "impact player" with no vertical leap. Michael's impact came from a gentle, giving spirit (that's the "love you, too" part), and from the maximum effort that he exerted to accomplish simple tasks.

The coach told the parents that he wanted Michael to hang around in the locker room to be a snapshot of love, respect and effort. Michael would lead the team onto the floor at home games. They would put their hands on him at center court and shout "1-2-3 Hawks!" and then start their pre-game warm-ups. Michael would sit behind the bench directly behind his new buddy, Coach Bollier.

I'd love to give you some kind of Hollywood ending to this story, about how the team won the state title, but that's not the way it played out. However, big strides were made. Everybody associated with the program saw "the value of *including others* in our quest."

For two parents who never thought that they would see the day their son, Michael, was a member of a sports team, it made a wonderful memory. For a team of high school basketball players, there were weekly lessons in maximum effort and having a heart for others. For a Georgia high school basketball coach transplanted from Indiana, it had been a "God-orchestrated" chance meeting with a child born in Romania, which would come to define the coach's program for the five years he coached there.

The night of the last home game, when the seniors were honored one by one, Michael was included in the festivities. He was announced last. As he drove his wheelchair to center court with his parents, the scene was heart-warming. Not only did the student body cheer, they raised their hands and made the "Love you, too" sign. My wife, Cheryl, and I will never forget that moment, because Michael is our son.

Phil Bollier went from being a total stranger to one of my best friends and a shining example of what Coach Wooden was all about. Wooden included a child that only he saw as an "impact player" as a model of teamwork. The experience reminded me of one of my favorite Scriptures, Philippians 2:3-5, in which Paul says, "Do nothing out of rivalry or conceit, but in humility consider others as more important than yourselves. Everyone should look out not [only] for his own interests, but also for the interests of others. Make your own attitude that of Christ Jesus."

That's not only my story. It's Michael's story. Phil's story. God's story.

WOODEN'S WISDOM

We can accomplish so much more when we work with others.

TRAINING TIME

1. How does "including others in our quest" demonstrate team-work?

2. Read Romans 12:4-6. How does this Scripture reinforce the importance of including others and working as a team?

3. Who is one person in your life that you can "include in your quest" and let him or her know their value to God?

PRAYER

Father, thank You for surrounding me with teammates that can teach me more about You and make my life better. Help me to consider them more important than myself and put their interests above my own. Help me to learn the value of teamwork and including others in the quest.

Ernie Johnson is the studio host for TNT Network's "Inside the NBA" and a two-time Sports Emmy Award winner. Johnson also hosts TNT's PGA Tour coverage and serves as a play-by-play announcer for Major League Baseball games on TBS.

The Simple Life

BY KYLE KORVER
NBA Guard, Utah Jazz

I've never stopped trying to do what's right.
JOHN WOODEN

I was born in Los Angeles where Coach Wooden's influence on the sports community was always evident. His name evoked reverence and respect. It was easy to be caught off guard by his demeanor and sometimes hard to imagine that he was such a great coach. Aren't coaches supposed to be fiery types that yell and scream? Not Coach Wooden. He was a consistent model of calm and poise.

Coach Wooden's legacy is a testament to sticking to the simple things. Tie your shoes right. Love one woman your whole life. Look at all the fruit he produced in his life because he focused on keeping it simple and doing right.

As a basketball player, I've found that sticking to the fundamentals helps me make good decisions in each game. As a shooting guard, one of my primary responsibilities is to score with the outside jump shot. The fundamentals include squaring up my shoulders to the basket, fully extending my arm before releasing the ball, following through after the shot, and being ready for the rebound or quickly getting back on defense. Staying focused on the simple things and doing them right has been one of the biggest keys to my success.

Not the most athletic guy on the floor, I've worked harder to get to this level than the majority of players. But it's important to remember, as Coach Wooden has said, that doing right isn't trying "to earn favor with God"—or with man for that matter. Doing right is a byproduct of having the proper perspective on your gifts and their purpose.

When I was in college, I'd stay up late or after practice to shoot around in the gym. It wasn't to impress the coach or be in good favor with him. I didn't just do it when he was around so he could hear the ball bouncing in the gym. I went because I loved it, it was fun and there was joy in it.

God's Word tells us that doing right is an important part of sharing the Gospel. In 1 Corinthians 9:27, Paul sets this example for us: "I discipline my body and bring it under strict control, so that after preaching to others, I myself will not be disqualified." In other words, doing things with integrity and resisting the temptation to cut corners will help maintain our Christian witness.

For me, that means surrounding myself with like-minded people—people that build me up, not tear me down. I've found that I eventually become like the people with whom I surround myself. As humans we're only so strong. If we put ourselves in enough bad situations, we will eventually fail. I've learned that lesson through many years of making good and bad decisions. If we focus on what's important and ask God for guidance, He will lead us and reveal His path.

Psalm 37:23 says, "A man's steps are established by the LORD, and He takes pleasure in his way." Once we understand that truth, it's a matter of simply putting one foot in front of the other.

That's the beauty of doing things the right way and keeping things simple. There's a reason why Coach Wooden was the greatest. In today's world with so many distractions, doing right isn't the easy thing to do. Coach Wooden led by following Christ's example. That's my goal as a believer, and I hope to inspire others in the same way Coach Wooden has inspired me.

WOODEN'S WISDOM

I'm not doing [right] to earn favor with God. I'm doing it because it's the right thing to do. My earthly father and my heavenly Father would expect nothing less.

TRAINING TIME

1. How can staying focused on the simple things and doing them right help you be successful in your family, work and daily life?

2. How can staying focused on the simple things and doing them right affect your daily walk with Christ?

3. Are you surrounding yourself with like-minded people that will help you do things with integrity and encourage you to follow Christ's purpose for your life?

PRAYER

Father, I know You have a specific purpose for my life. Help me to focus on the things that are the most important and do them with integrity. Help me to follow Your example and walk the path You've laid out for me, one step at a time.

Kyle Korver is a shooting guard who plays for the NBA's Utah Jazz. At Creighton University, he set a Missouri Valley Conference record with 371 career three-pointers and was twice named MVC Player of the Year. Korver also became Creighton's first player to appear in four consecutive NCAA Tournaments.

The Greatest Word

BY ANTHONY MUÑOZ

Hall of Fame NFL Lineman, Cincinnati Bengals

"Love" is the greatest word in our language.

JOHN WOODEN

Coach Wooden described "love" as the greatest word in our language. I would also say that love is also the greatest gift. Coach Wooden spent most of his life giving that gift freely to everyone who was blessed to know him.

For me, that opportunity came a few short years ago at a breakfast where both Coach Wooden and I were among the guests. When I introduced myself to him, he quickly responded and said, "Oh, I know who you are! You played at USC!"

I was taken aback that he would remember me. My college playing days had ended 25 years earlier. But something else struck me and has stayed with me ever since. Coach Wooden's eyes reflected love. Even those who didn't know he was a man of great faith would have noticed something different about him. But I was already aware of his love for the LORD and his love for people. That face-to-face meeting only confirmed it.

I'm also a firm believer in Coach Wooden's belief that, "When we have love, many of our problems disappear." He modeled that kind of love and respect for his players, a diverse group of young men that he brought together for one common goal. Coach Wooden often cites his 1970 championship team as such a group with very different players like Henry Bibby and John Vallely, whom he brought together for the purpose of proving they could win even without a big man like Lew Alcindor, who graduated the year before, to dominate in the paint.

When you hear them talk about Coach Wooden today, it's clear that playing for him was a life-changing experience. And it all started with love—love for God, love for family, love for his players, and love for the game of basketball.

I too have learned to exercise that kind of love in my life. It's the basis for everything I do with my family and all that I hope to accomplish through the Muñoz Foundation. We bring kids from different backgrounds together and we teach them to show love and respect for one another, and in the process we begin to eliminate a lot of society's problems.

Part of giving love to others is helping them see their potential. The kids we work with have been given tremendous gifts, but they need someone to love on them and encourage them to build their confidence. If we can help families financially, maybe we can be that boost to help those kids succeed and go on to finish high school or college.

It's very easy at times to ask, "Why do it? Why go to all the trouble?" But then I am quickly reminded of what Paul writes in Galatians 6:9: "Let us not become weary in doing good" (*NIV*). When love is at the center of your actions, you won't get tired of doing good things for others. That's because true love gives us the strength to continue on even when our bodies get tired and our flesh wants to give up. How do we know if we're operating with true, God-centered love? I like to use 1 Corinthians 13:4-8 as my guide:

Love is patient; love is kind. Love does not envy; is not boastful; is not conceited; does not act improperly; is not selfish; is not provoked; does not keep a record of wrongs; finds no joy in unrighteousness, but rejoices in the truth; bears all things, believes all things, hopes all things, endures all things. Love never ends.

Love puts others before ourselves and doesn't look for accolades. It's a matter of being obedient to God. That's how I hope love is played out in my words and actions.

"Love" meant something to Coach Wooden, and it means something to me. It's about the very essence of God and what He has done for us. I've been walking with the Lord for 30 years now, and I still can't fathom how God was able to give His only Son for my sins. I can't imagine sacrificing my son, Michael, for anyone else. So when God says He loves us, He really means it. He demonstrated that love for us when He allowed Jesus to die on the cross.

The love I show for my family, my friends and my community pales in comparison to God's love. But His amazing gift does challenge me to take the love He has placed in my heart and share it with others.

Coach Wooden was an inspiration because he loved others and freely gave of his time and his wisdom as often as he could. When I last saw him, it was evident that people were attracted to his spirit. Everyone was hanging on his every word. After all those years, he was still a powerful example of love. There is no reason why I can't follow his example and live my life by the words of 1 John 4:7-8:

Dear friends, let us love one another, for love comes from God. Everyone who loves has been born of God and knows God (NIV).

WOODEN'S WISDOM

*When we have love, many of our problems disappear.
Differences are manageable when love has its way. . . . We can
give without loving, but we can't love without giving. In fact,
love is nothing unless we give it to someone.*

TRAINING TIME

1. How is love the greatest word in our language and the greatest gift you can give others?

2. Read 1 Corinthians 13:4-8. Are you demonstrating God-centered love in your life?

3. What are some practical things that you can do to show God-centered love to those around you?

PRAYER

*Father, thank You for the gift of love. Help me to
incorporate God-centered love into every aspect of my life and
show Your love to my family, friends and community. I want
to be a vessel of Your love to everyone I meet!*

Anthony Muñoz is a member of the Pro Football Hall of Fame. He was an 11-time All-Pro offensive lineman who played 13 seasons with the Cincinnati Bengals. Muñoz resides in Cincinnati where he runs the Anthony Muñoz Foundation.

Noble Goals

BY SUE SEMRAU

Head Coach, Women's Basketball, Florida State University

*I believe we are most likely to succeed when ambition
is focused on noble and worthy purposes and outcomes
rather than on goals set out of selfishness.*

JOHN WOODEN

Early in my career as a Division I basketball coach, if you'd asked me what my ultimate goal for my team was, I would have given you one response: an NCAA championship.

I wouldn't give you the same answer today. Don't get me wrong. As a highly competitive person, I enjoy nothing more than helping my players achieve material success on the basketball court. But that is no longer at the crux of who I am.

Since I've grown in my relationship with Christ, I've come to understand what it means to have more "noble goals" like Coach Wooden talks about in his Pyramid of Success. My ambition has shifted over the years towards fulfilling "worthy purposes and outcomes rather than on goals set out of selfishness."

It all started to change shortly after I became a Christian. During that time, I was the women's basketball coach at Occidental College. Through a dear friend, Debbie Haliday, I was given the opportunity to meet with Coach Wooden in his home. Debbie was a member of UCLA's 1978 AIAW national championship team and was instrumental in leading me to Christ.

As a young coach and a very young Christian, I had a different idea about success. Success, to me, was worldly success. Coach Wooden and Debbie both had the success I wanted. But as I looked at their lives, I saw that their success wasn't based on anything the world had to offer. Coach Wooden, like me, was highly competitive. He had a strong desire to win. But his emphasis was first and foremost on improving as a coach and helping his players improve as a team and as young men. I began to understand that the success I saw in Coach and Debbie was an outflow of their relationship with Jesus Christ.

That's when my life turned from desiring the things of this world to desiring the things of His kingdom. God changed me. Psalm 37:4 took on new meaning in my life: "Take delight in the LORD, and He will give you your heart's desires."

Before then, I desired a national championship, so I felt that God would give me that desire. But instead, He helped me understand that it's not my desires He wants to give me, but rather the desires that He has placed in my heart.

In many ways, I can relate to the apostle Paul. Before he became the most famous evangelist of all time, he had a different name—Saul of Tarsus. Saul was a religious zealot who opposed the Jews who were turning to Christianity after Jesus' death and resurrection. He relentlessly pursued, persecuted and even executed many members of the Early Church.

And then Saul encountered God in a miraculous fashion. He was traveling to Damascus when a light from the sky blinded him and stopped him in his tracks. Saul heard God's voice and was instantly transformed. He changed his name to Paul and went on to etch his name in history as the Church's most powerful leader. But that didn't come without a heavy price. Paul went through a series of hardships such as imprisonment, whippings, beatings and exile.

Like Paul, my faith journey came with some hardships that continued to shape my life's ambitions. One such instance took place during the 2004 season at Florida State. Three years earlier, we made it to our first NCAA tournament in 10 years. The next two seasons were mediocre, and we failed to get back to the NCAA Tournament and settled for a pair of WNIT bids. My job was probably on the line.

During the offseason, expectations were high. We were excited about Ronalda Pierce, whom I felt was destined to be an All-American and potential WNBA star. Her 6' 5" frame gave her a dominating edge in the paint. I believed this was the year we would get back to the NCAA Tournament.

That's when everything changed. On June 8, I got a phone call at three o'clock in the morning. Ronalda had been rushed to the hospital and died of an aortic aneurysm that resulted from a rare genetic disorder called Marfan syndrome.

Her death shook the very foundation of who we were as a team. Things were already very difficult, and we lost our starting point guard for the season to a pregnancy. Through that time, an amazing transformation took place. The 2004 team won more games than any other team at Florida State in 10 years and started a six-year run at the NCAA Tournament.

By the end of the season, I had been named ACC Coach of the Year, but truthfully, it had nothing to do with me. We obtained worldly success, but the most important thing for me was the lessons I learned about building relationships with my players.

My thinking was challenged again during the 2010 NCAA Tournament. Florida State advanced to its first ever Elite Eight and won a school-record 29 games. Then we played the University of Connecticut squad that finished the season 39-0 and with a 78-game winning streak. The Lady Huskies handed us a devastating 90-50 loss en route to its fourth consecutive national championship.

As I prepared to talk to the team after the game, I was reminded of a summer trip our team had taken to South Africa a few months earlier. When I walked in, here's what I said: "I want you to take yourself back to that village in Kayamandi where we led the basketball clinic. Those kids didn't have shoes. Those kids didn't know where their next meal was coming from. Did those things define them? No! And this loss doesn't define you. You've continued to build your character, give selflessly and humble yourselves. That's who you are. That's what defines you. Not what happened in this game tonight."

I wanted to explain to my players the truth that I've discovered about ambition. The key to having right ambitions and noble goals means having a right perspective of success. As Coach Wooden has said, success is "knowing you did your best to become the best you are capable of becoming."

When your ambition is directed towards that end, you'll find yourself putting others first and existing for the purpose of fulfilling God's will for your life.

WOODEN'S WISDOM

If our ambition is to be highly publicized, receive a lot of recognition, attain a position of power or prestige, or make a lot of money, we do not have noble goals. If we are focused away from ourselves and on the team and others, we possess noble goals.

TRAINING TIME

1. Read Psalm 37:4. Does your heart desire worldly success or what God desires?

2. What are some current goals that you have that are for selfish desires?

3. How can you change these self-centered goals into noble goals?

PRAYER

Father, please forgive me when I desire worldly success over the things You desire for me. Help me to focus on worthy and noble purposes and outcomes for my life.

Sue Semrau is the women's basketball coach at Florida State University, where she has won more games than any other coach in school history. Semrau was named the 2004, 2007 and 2009 ACC Coach of the Year and currently serves on the Board of Directors for the Women's Basketball Coaches Association.

Under Control

BY JUNIOR BRIDGEMAN

Former NBA Forward-Guard, Milwaukee Bucks and
Los Angeles Clippers

*Self-control is the ability to discipline ourselves and keep
our emotions under control.*

JOHN WOODEN

There have been only a few things in my life that I've said were
truly worth sharing with my grandkids someday. One of those
moments happened on March 6, 2009, when I was inducted into
the Missouri Valley Conference Hall of Fame at a special ceremony in St. Louis, Missouri. Perhaps more significant than the
award itself is the person who introduced me at the ceremony.

Each of the inductees was introduced by a presentation
video, and mine contained surprise commentary from none
other than Coach Wooden, who was also being inducted that
day as a former coach at Indiana State. His kind words were very
unexpected. It was startling to hear him recall coaching against
me and remembering me as a good player, especially considering
all of the great players he coached.

That video message from Coach Wooden was as special as
anything that's ever happened to me as a basketball player, be-

cause he has been the epitome of so many values and principles that I hold dear.

Self-control is one such character trait that Coach Wooden modeled throughout his storied coaching career. This trait has been an important part of my success as a basketball player and now as a businessman.

I didn't have the opportunity to play for Coach Wooden, but at Louisville I experienced the next best thing with Coach Denny Crum, who cut his teeth as an assistant coach at UCLA. I played for Coach Crum when he took over the Cardinals basketball program in 1971, and I vicariously learned from Coach Wooden through his example.

People might think it's easy to be calm and collected when you're winning 88 games in a row like the Bruins did, but it's not. When you're a coach, it's never easy. Things happen in games that make you want to react emotionally. Many coaches tend to yell and scream. Not Coach Wooden. He always sat calmly and stayed focused on his job—coaching his team and using every moment to teach his players something important about basketball and life.

Coach Wooden's example reminds me of how Jesus interacted with the disciples. So often they had trouble understanding His teachings and sometimes flat out rejected His prophetic words. And yet Jesus calmly stepped back and allowed them to learn the hard way.

One such instance can be found in Luke 22. While gathered for that Last Supper, Jesus did His best to prepare the disciples for what was to come. Just a few hours away from His crucifixion, He told Simon Peter that he would deny his LORD three times before the rooster crowed three times (verse 34). Peter rejected this notion. When it happened and Jesus encountered him after His Resurrection, Jesus didn't say, "You see? I told you so! You did it!"

As humans, our first reaction is to cast blame and point out to others that we were right and they were wrong. Yet, in a situation where Jesus was completely justified in rebuking Peter, He exercised self-control. Jesus knew Peter better than he knew himself. He wasn't surprised when Peter caved in to his fear. So He had no problem showing compassion instead of condemnation.

Coach Wooden displayed that same kind of self-control when his UCLA team played North Carolina State in the 1974 national championship game. Years later, Bill Walton shared with me how that group of players was probably as close to being un-coachable as you would ever see on one of Coach Wooden's teams.

As the game started to get out of control, Bill called a time-out. Coach just said to them, "You guys have tried to do it your way all along, so go ahead and just do it your way." The Bruins ended up losing the game 80-77 in double overtime after giving up a pair of big leads. The loss broke a string of seven consecutive national championships.

Coach Wooden could have gotten caught up in the frustrating moment, but instead he maintained his self-control and his players learned a hard lesson as a result of their stubbornness. Like Christ, Coach Wooden understood the power of emotions. If we control our emotions, we can control our words and actions.

The first step to self-control is to admit that we can't do it on our own. We must live a life that is, as Galatians 5:18 says, "led by the spirit" and marked by the fruit of the spirit found in Galatians 5:22-23: "love, joy, peace, patience, kindness, goodness, faithfulness, gentleness, and self-control."

I can think of very few people in my lifetime whose lives completely matched what they professed. Coach Wooden sits alone at the top of that list. His example as a spirit-led man of great discipline and self-control should serve as an inspiration to us all.

WOODEN'S WISDOM

To become our best, good judgment and common sense are essential.
No matter the task—whether physical or mental—if our emotions take
over, we're not going to execute near our personal level of competency,
because both judgment and common sense will be impaired. When our
emotions dominate our actions, we make mistakes.

TRAINING TIME

1. Have you ever been in a situation where you let your emotions take control and caused you to act wrongly?

2. How would thinking about a situation from the other person's perspective help you choose the right response?

3. Is there a situation in your life currently where you can exercise self-control by showing compassion instead of condemnation? If so, what is it?

4. Read Galatians 5:16-26. How does exercising self-control show you're living by the Spirit and not your own desires?

PRAYER

Father, please forgive me for choosing to follow my emotions
and my own sinful nature in situations. Help me to live by the
Spirit and exercise self-control in my daily life.

Junior Bridgeman is the president of Bridgeman Foods LLC, a company that owns and operates several restaurant franchises across the country. He previously spent 12 years in the NBA with the Milwaukee Bucks and the Los Angeles Clippers. An All-American at the University of Louisville, Bridgeman earned back-to-back Missouri Valley Conference Player of the Year honors and was inducted into the MVC Hall of Fame.

The Power of Patience

BY DEB PATTERSON
Head Coach, Women's Basketball, Kansas State University

Patience is the ability to wait and calmly persevere.
JOHN WOODEN

Rarely are you in the presence of someone who is so sincerely interested in the moment that time stands still. But that's the best way I can describe being with Coach Wooden. He exuded incredible patience as he lived in the moment sincerely, openly and warmly. Coach Wooden didn't know me when I first spent time with him in his home during the summer of 2007, but he had the patience and compassion to make it a special moment for both of us.

I can't say I have the same level of patience, but that's certainly not God's fault. He's been trying to teach me patience for the better part of 30 years now. My long and winding journey started back in 1982 when I took my first job at Hononegah High School in Rockton, Illinois, a neighboring town of Rockford where I grew up and attended Rockford College.

When I started as the girls' basketball coach and physical education teacher, there was a certain level of hope that I could make a difference in a very difficult environment. The program was in disarray and had gone winless for the previous three seasons. And there were some very difficult young people on the team.

The ugly truth reared its head about two weeks into the school year. I walked into the locker room and discovered four of my players engaged in a physical altercation. One of these girls was a nationally ranked judo athlete. Imagine my horror at the sight of a mixed martial arts catfight!

After breaking up the fight, I went home and evaluated what I needed to do to change the toxic culture in the locker room. That's when I decided to start with Coach Wooden's Pyramid of Success as the foundation for Hononegah girls' basketball. I bought some white poster board and drew up my own version of the Pyramid. I included them in our team notebook, and I would meet with the girls and go over every block and mortar quality. Not only did it become the framework for those players, it also became the framework of hope, guidance and purpose for me as their head coach.

So what does this story have to do with patience? Everything. After I took the team through these principles and values, the culture, personality, character and expectations of the team began to change. So, what happened that first season? We went 0-22. The team was determined to press on. The following year, we won three games. The year after that, we won 17 games. In my fourth season at Hononegah, our team won an astounding 21 games en route to a conference championship and advanced to the state's regional basketball tournament.

Not only did those girls learn some important life lessons, but I was forever changed. The patience I developed through that four-year experience has carried over into my career at Kansas State. In the times I feel overwhelmed, I think about the principle of patience from Coach Wooden that is reinforced by God's Word. One of my favorite Scriptures is Isaiah 40:29-31, which says:

He gives strength to the weary and strengthens the powerless. Youths may faint and grow weary, and young men stumble and fall, but those who trust in the LORD will renew their strength; they will soar on wings like eagles; they will run and not grow weary; they will walk and not faint.

So often we get weak in our faith and then we get impatient. Our impatience makes us lose our resolve. If we keep our hope in the LORD, then He will help us make right decisions instead of taking shortcuts or, even worse, giving up altogether.

In the Bible, we can look to Daniel as an example of someone who exercised patience and reaped great benefits and blessings. Daniel was snatched away from his family by the Babylonians and sequestered with other young men. King Nebuchadnezzar tried to brainwash him and his friends with a perverted form of wisdom and assimilate them into a pagan culture. Yet Daniel resisted those temptations by resting in God's sovereignty and trusting in the fact that he was there for a divine purpose.

If Daniel had not been patient with God's plan, his resolve would have been weakened and he would not have taken such a bold stand to stay true to his convictions. And this wasn't a one-time decision. Daniel had to make that choice every day as he dealt with life's twists and turns. He relied on his patience in dealing with three different kings and the dubious plots of jealous men that sometimes meant literally standing face to face with lions.

Sometimes we can get tossed into a proverbial den of lions and the only thing we can do is trust God. Proverbs 3:5-6 reminds us of that truth: "Trust in the LORD with all your heart, and do not rely on your own understanding; think about Him in all your ways, and He will guide you on the right paths."

If trust is at the core of your relationship with God, then it won't matter how long it takes for you to get where He's taking you. When you direct your life toward trusting in the LORD, He will give you the character and patience to wait on His eternal purpose.

And here's the best part. God will be patient with you even when you lack patience and are on the verge of giving up. As it says in 2 Peter 3:9, "The Lord does not delay His promise, as some understand delay, but is patient with you, not wanting any to perish, but all to come to repentance."

What an awesome promise! I've seen that exhibited in Coach Wooden's life, and I'm challenged to see evidence of it in mine too. It's true. Patience *is* a virtue. And it will breed excellence in all areas of our world.

WOODEN'S WISDOM

Often the element of time adds value to an accomplishment. Good things take time, as they should. We shouldn't expect good things to happen overnight.

TRAINING TIME

1. Have you been through a difficult circumstance that God used to teach you patience?

2. Read Isaiah 40:29-31. How does this Scripture give you encouragement to have patience and press on through difficult circumstances?

3. Is trust at the core of your relationship with God?

PRAYER

Father, help me to be patient with Your plan for my life.
In the midst of difficult circumstances, help me to trust in You
and lean on You for strength and guidance as You build me
into the person You want me to be.

Deb Patterson is the women's basketball coach at Kansas State University and a two-time Big 12 Coach of the Year. She has led the Wildcats to seven NCAA Tournament appearances through 2010 and a pair of Big 12 championships. Kansas State also won the 2006 WNIT title under her guidance.

Slow and Steady

BY BRUCE WEBER

Head Coach, Men's Basketball, University of Illinois

Most people have a tendency to look for shortcuts or at least for the easiest way to complete any given task.

JOHN WOODEN

When John Wooden was coaching, he would rise early and go for a morning walk. The walks were lengthy, allowing time for reflecting, planning and building relationships with those who joined him on the daily journey. I've had the privilege to join Coach on some of those walks.

I was fortunate to meet John Wooden at a Medalist clinic in Louisville when I was still a young college student. My good friend, who was a note taker for the clinics, had befriended Coach Wooden. That week we got up early and took the long, steady walk with him. I didn't say much on those walks. I just listened and learned. Those times taught me so much about life and my career as a coach. In fact, I can relate what I learned on those walks to the famous line in Aesop's fable, *The Tortoise and the Hare*, "slow and steady wins the race."

For me, the "slow" part of that equation is all about patience. I spent 18 years as an assistant coach for Gene Keady at Purdue

University. At first, I was one of the youngest assistants in the Big Ten. After a while, I became one of the nation's longest-running assistants. It wasn't for lack of trying. You can't imagine how many places I interviewed. Take a college directory and stick a pin in any random page. I probably interviewed there—maybe even twice!

As far as the "steady" element, that speaks to the issue of integrity. In my 18 years with Coach Keady, we regularly made the NCAA Tournament and won six Big Ten championships. There were other assistant coaches that jumped by me and made the leap into head coaching positions. Along the way, I started to wonder if there was some other avenue to get to my desired destination. But I stuck with my beliefs and enjoyed an unbelievable run at Purdue. I couldn't be more proud of what we accomplished there.

Even as I was doing my best to stand my ground, there were people who came to me and said, "You need to go after that job over there." And I'd reply, "But that coach hasn't even been fired yet!" I was amazed that while I was trying to work on scouting reports and perform my job to the best of my ability, there were people actually implying that I should cut corners to achieve my goals. But in the long haul, my patience and virtue ended up paying off for me.

I saw that same principle of staying true to godly beliefs modeled in the life of my hero, Coach Wooden. Over time, I found that Coach Wooden was a man of great integrity. He didn't take shortcuts. Instead, he always held to his values and his beliefs. From a distance, I caught a glimpse of the way it should be done.

And that carried over into my job as a head coach. My first opportunity came in 1998 when I took the reins at Southern Illinois. Even there I could have left after the first year. In fact, every year I was there I could have left for another job. But I told the administration that I was going to stay there until we got the program going. I promised that I wouldn't accept another job unless it was one they would be proud of me to take.

Five years later and on the heels of back-to-back NCAA Tournament appearances, that opportunity finally came. After a series of coaching changes that involved Roy Williams leaving Kansas for North Carolina and Bill Self leaving Illinois for Kansas, I was hired to be the Fighting Illini's next head coach.

The Bible tells the story of another man who took a slow and steady path to the finish line. His name was Joseph, and he is considered one of history's greatest examples of longsuffering and integrity. Joseph had 11 brothers, but he was his father, Jacob's, favorite son. The others were extremely jealous, so they threw him in a pit, faked his death and sold him into slavery.

Joseph's owner, a man named Potiphar, eventually elevated him to be the superintendent of his household. But when Joseph resisted the sexual advances of Potiphar's wife, he was falsely accused of attacking her and was sent to prison. Still, God was faithful to Joseph because of his integrity, and while in jail he was put in charge of the other prisoners.

Two years later, God used Joseph to interpret the pharaoh's troubling dreams and was freed from prison and appointed to be the viceroy of Egypt. Joseph's interpretations ultimately saved the nation from famine. In the process, he was able to reconcile with his brothers and save his family from starvation, too. But none of that would have happened if Joseph had compromised his godly principles. He was strong in his convictions and relied on God's strength to make the difficult, but right choices.

That's my goal in life. I want to live a life of integrity that is pleasing to God. When I go to bed at night, I don't have to worry about a lie I told. I don't have to worry about my wife of nearly 30 years and my three daughters reading about me in the paper. I can feel good knowing that both my reputation and my good name are secure.

Nobody is perfect. We all know that. I'm sure somewhere in there, even Coach Wooden had some faults. Yet looking at the life of Joseph and the modern example of Coach Wooden shows you the power of a legacy.

Anyone can build that same kind of heritage for the future. It will probably require a slow and steady approach, but getting to the finish line and doing it with integrity is well worth the effort.

WOODEN'S WISDOM

Today, in sports and in most areas of life, many people adopt a win-at-all-costs stance. Our media and popular culture bolster this approach. . . . I maintain that there is no end to living a win-at-all-costs life and, when we follow this course, we find that we have no peace of mind.

TRAINING TIME

1. Have you ever experienced a time when it seemed like opportunities were passing you by and you were tempted to take shortcuts to achieve your goals?

2. How does having integrity and patience help you achieve your goals the right way?

3. Read the account of Joseph's life in Genesis 37, 39–47. How did God bless Joseph for not compromising his godly principles?

PRAYER

Father, please forgive me when I have compromised my integrity to achieve a goal. Help me to hold fast to godly principles and the plan You have for me, even when it takes time to see the results.

Bruce Weber is the men's basketball coach at the University of Illinois where he has led the Illini to five NCAA Tournament appearances, two Big Ten regular season titles and a Big Ten Tournament championship in his first seven seasons there. In 2005, Weber was named Naismith and Associated Press National Coach of the Year and Big Ten Coach of the Year.

Marked by Passion

BY MIKE SINGLETARY
Head Coach, San Francisco 49ers

Enthusiasm brushes off upon those with whom you come in contact.
JOHN WOODEN

Coach Wooden may not have been an exuberant, emotional man, but he displayed enthusiasm in every detail of coaching. A lot of people think enthusiasm is all about screaming, yelling and jumping around, but Coach Wooden taught me that enthusiasm has nothing to do with outward physical expression. Enthusiasm is marked by passion.

Coach Wooden was passionate about investing in his players. Somehow, someway, he was going to touch a life. He modeled consistency in the little things. He knew how to make them champions on the basketball court, but he also wanted to make them champions in the way they dressed, in the way they carried themselves, in the way they treated their girlfriends or wives, and in the way they made a contribution to their community. The only way Coach Wooden could instill that was to convey it through his own life. In return, his players caught his vision and became enthusiastic members of his team.

His enthusiasm for coaching has bled over into my career. I want to do my best to model enthusiasm to my players and my assistant coaches. That means preaching the importance of consistency and commitment.

I often think back to 1984 when I was playing with the Chicago Bears. Early in the year, we were talking about being a playoff team and going to the Super Bowl. After a 3-0 start, things were looking good. But then our team endured some key injuries and the occasional internal dispute. After a home loss to the Dallas Cowboys, many players began to doubt whether we were ready to be a playoff contender. It was our second loss in a row, and we had the look of a team that lacked confidence.

That next week, several guys in the locker room conveyed that very thought to me in private. But I knew what I believed in my heart, mind and soul. We were ready, but our team just didn't believe it. We had a fear of success.

At practice, the five team captains stood before the team and led the warm-up exercises. It came my time to lead the team in pushups. As I looked at our guys, I made a decision that I wasn't going to let my team give up. I passionately addressed them with tears in my eyes. "I refuse to go home early this year!" I told them. "I'm tired of watching other teams in the playoffs!"

When I was done, it was very quiet for what seemed like a long, long time. And then one of our star defensive players, Dan Hampton, started clapping . . . and then everybody started clapping. The team made a turn that day, and from that point on, we won seven of our last 11 games. We advanced to the NFC championship where we lost to the San Francisco 49ers. But the next year, we went all the way to Super Bowl XX and won.

That story reminds me of Joshua and Caleb's situation in Numbers 13. God had told Moses to send 12 spies to explore the land that He had promised them. Of those 12 men, 10 of them returned this report: "There is no way that we have a chance! We look like grasshoppers compared to these people! They look like giants! Their cities are fortified with tall walls!"

But Joshua and Caleb were enthusiastic about God's promise to them. In Numbers 13:30 we see their enthusiasm displayed: "Then Caleb quieted the people in the presence of Moses and said, 'We must go up and take possession of the land because we can certainly conquer it!'"

Joshua and Caleb sound like the kind of players I want on my team. They didn't believe in how things appeared; they believed what God had said. That's where enthusiasm is so important. It gives you the ability to see through the junk and catch a glimpse of God's vision for your life.

Coach Wooden modeled that kind of enthusiasm at UCLA when he bucked the trends and created his own way of coaching. He had a passion for his players, for his family, for his God and for his game. It showed in every little thing he did.

That's the kind of enthusiasm I want to bring to my life every day. And like Coach Wooden, I want my example to rub off on those around me, so they too can experience the same passion for life and for God that drives me to be the best I can be.

WOODEN'S WISDOM

You must truly enjoy what you are doing.

TRAINING TIME

1. Do you know someone who displays real enthusiasm in his or her life?

2. Read Numbers 13. How did Caleb and Joshua show enthusiasm for God's promise?

3. What steps can you take to be more enthusiastic in the work God has given you to do?

PRAYER

Father, I want to have enthusiasm for the work You have given me to accomplish, even in the smallest details. Show me a glimpse of Your vision and give me a passion to see it carried out in my life.

Mike Singletary is head coach of the San Francisco 49ers and a member of the Pro Football Hall of Fame. Singletary played 12 seasons with the Chicago Bears, where he was a member of the Super Bowl XX championship team. He was selected to 10 Pro Bowls and was twice named NFL Defensive Player of the Year. He is the co-author, with Jay Carty, of *Mike Singletary One-on-One*.

Working It Out

BY DR. JIM REEVE

Senior Pastor, Faith Community Church, West Covina, California

---

Worthwhile results come from hard work and careful planning.

JOHN WOODEN

What do Coach Wooden's 10 national championships have in common with Faith Community Church in West Covina, California, the church I launched with a handful of people in 1980, which now averages 10,000 attendees a week? At first glance, it may seem like there's not much in common. However, my hero and role model in ministry is not a saint from Church history or a contemporary leader of a mega-ministry but a basketball coach. Whatever success I may have achieved in ministry is due in no small part to principles taught and modeled by Coach Wooden.

The first association with Coach Wooden is part of a familiar story that you hear often throughout Southern California. Just like many other teenagers back in the mid to late '60s, I was a UCLA basketball fanatic. My friends and I were always careful to be home by 11 o'clock to watch that night's tape-delayed game. I can still hear the "oh my" of famed sports broadcaster Dick Enberg as a seemingly endless stream of spectacular shots would win yet another game for the Bruins.

But for me, the thrill of victory and unprecedented success were not really what it was all about. It had much more to do with Coach Wooden and the principles he espoused at a time when the world seemed obsessed with fame, celebrity and money. Coach Wooden rose above the times and, like heroes do, influenced the times. He influenced me.

My son and I had the opportunity to meet my hero a few years ago. It was a thrill to interact face to face with the person who had impacted my life from a distance more than most had from up close. To this day when people ask me what the key has been to our church's success, I tell them, "Well, it's the Pyramid of Success."

One block from the Pyramid that has especially inspired me is Coach Wooden's teaching on industriousness, something I've tried to incorporate ever since God used me to start Faith Community Church. Coach Wooden always talked about what was really important in sports and in life. To him, it was not about the score or winning or losing; the outcome was merely the byproduct of preparation and hard work.

Similarly, ministry is not about attendance numbers or the size of the offerings, but about growing disciples of Jesus. I have never focused on trying to build a big and successful church; I have always focused on trying to build successful Christians. A large church has simply been a byproduct.

Christians can sometimes get hung up when you start talking about hard work. Maybe that's because the word "work" can smack of ideas that seem contrary to faith. After all, we're saved not by works but by faith. But does having faith mean that we don't have to work? When I run across that issue, I point to Philippians 2:12, where Paul writes, "So then, my dear friends, just as you have always obeyed, not only in my presence, but now even more in my absence, work out your own salvation with fear and trembling."

If you don't read this verse carefully, it sounds as if Paul is saying that you've got to work for your salvation. But Paul isn't saying that. You don't work *for* your salvation; you work *out* your salvation. When you go into training, you're working out. You can only work out what God has already worked into you.

If I work hard to be like someone else rather than working out what is in me, the result can be disastrous. Joel Osteen is a friend and fellow pastor, who also happens to lead the largest church in America. Now, that is success! But if I were to think that for me to be successful I had to work hard to preach and lead like Joel, I would be making a huge mistake. I'm not called to be like Joel Osteen. I'm called to work out who God has called me to be.

Working for your salvation, rather than working out what is in you, can lead to a performance-based life. I had more than one coach over the years try to motivate our team with the old adage, "Winning is not everything; it is the only thing." This is not what Coach Wooden meant by hard work and careful planning. Industriousness is not about the score; it's about the process of being the best you can be.

When I think about industriousness, my mind travels back to the days of the Early Church. One of my favorite heroes from the New Testament is Barnabas. Surprised? Yet without Barnabas, we would not have much of the New Testament. Why is that? Because Barnabas encouraged the church in Jerusalem to accept Paul into their fellowship.

Before his conversion, Paul, then called Saul, was ruthlessly persecuting Christians. The Church was skeptical about the genuineness of his conversion and understandably apprehensive about allowing him into their midst. Barnabas courageously stood up for Paul and testified to the authenticity of his faith. Without the courage and encouragement of Barnabas, the letters of Paul that make up much of the New Testament may have never been written.

Eventually, Paul ended up passing Barnabas in renown. A lot of guys in ministry today would be jealous if someone they helped get started in ministry became more popular than them. Not Barnabas. He was more interested in doing the Lord's work than in personal accolades. He was an industrious hard worker who was content to run the race in the lane God had set for him.

Barnabas understood something profound about success: It's about giving your best and letting God take care of who gets credit in the end. Maybe Paul was thinking of his mentor Barnabas when he wrote in Galatians 6:4-5, "Don't compare yourself with others. Each of you must take responsibility for doing the creative best you can with your own life" (*THE MESSAGE*).

That's not an easy concept to accept in our performance-driven world that thrives on materialism, power and fame. Nonetheless, I've come to learn that it's about working out—not working for—God's gifts in our life that brings real joy and peace. All you have to do is look at Coach Wooden's life to see the fruit of industriousness and a right perspective of success.

WOODEN'S WISDOM
I've always wanted to be the best I can be. I still do, so I work at it.

TRAINING TIME

1. Read Philippians 2:12. Why does Paul encourage us to "work out" our salvation?

2. Why is it sometimes difficult to not want to receive credit for something you worked hard on?

3. What steps can you take to be more industrious in your daily life and in your relationship with Christ?

PRAYER

*Father, help me to work out my salvation every day
so that I can be the person You called me to be. Help me to
avoid the performance-driven mentality but focus on the
process of the journey that You've laid before me.*

Dr. Jim Reeve is senior pastor and founder of Faith Community Church in West Covina, California. He is a published author, and his television program, *Balanced Living*, airs both nationally and internationally. Dr. Reeve earned his master's and PhD from Fuller Theological Seminary.

Disciplined to Win

BY MARV DUNPHY

Head Coach, Men's Volleyball, Pepperdine University

We discipline ourselves so someone else does not have to.
JOHN WOODEN

When you spend time with someone who is successful, often you find out that there are many outside influences that made him or her great. But the closer I got to Coach Wooden, the more I realized that I was in the presence of greatness. It wasn't Westwood. It wasn't UCLA. It wasn't the Pac-10. It was John Wooden.

In 1979, I was working on my Doctorate in Education and decided to do my dissertation on Coach Wooden. The title of the study was, "John Robert Wooden: The Coaching Process." When I introduced myself, he surprised me by saying, "Marv, I know who you are. We met at Pepperdine one day outside the pool at the gym."

Coach Wooden was a great listener, and of all his skills, that one was right there at the top. I introduced my idea in one breath, because I didn't want him to say no. He paused for a moment and then said something that surprised me even more:

"To be quite frank, I am honored that somebody of your caliber would want to do this on me."

Of course, I was the one who was truly honored that Coach Wooden would allow me so much access into his great coaching mind. For several days, I went to his home and asked over a hundred questions, and I received hours of audiotaped responses in return.

One day I asked Coach Wooden about discipline. I was curious as to how this legendary coach took care of problems both on and off the court. What he said has stuck with me ever since: "I never wanted to bruise the dignity of the one who was being disciplined." I wonder how many coaches, parents, teachers or leaders today can say that they live by that philosophy.

Coach Wooden also emphasized that individuals never lose the desire to be treated as individuals. He was great at understanding each player and using the proper mode of correction for each one based on his or her personality. This idea is something that I have tried to implement in my coaching over time.

He also taught me that how you say no as a parent, teacher or coach is much more important than how you say yes. It's easy to say yes, but the way you tell someone no can set the tone for the rest of that relationship. Coach Wooden never wavered when it was time to administer discipline, but he did it with respect. I caught a glimpse of this during our time together. When I would ask him a question, he would give it to me straight.

More importantly, Coach Wooden modeled self-discipline. He lived it out in real time for his players to observe daily. It's not what you say; it's what you do. And Coach Wooden was disciplined in everything he did. I never heard him make an excuse in any way, shape, or form.

He was also disciplined in how he balanced his work life with his home life. The key to his success was simple. He didn't bring his work home. One day I asked his wife, Nell, if Coach Wooden ever worked from home or even talked about his work in the evenings. She flatly said, "Never."

I curiously asked Coach about this, and he told me that he discussed all work-related matters with his staff and his trainer and good friend Ducky Drake, but never with Nell.

What happened at home during the day was more important than anything that happened with him during his day at work. And he really meant it.

Coach Wooden inspired me to live a disciplined life. This is important for leaders of any level of influence, especially coaches. As you model discipline, it becomes a reflection of your team. You have to be consistent and treat people the same every day. When you do that, they know where you stand. I think people knew where Coach Wooden stood. He may have adapted a little over time, but he was a model of consistency throughout his career and life.

One of the things that I've found to be true about most of the successful teams that I've coached at both the NCAA and Olympic levels is that they have had the ability to consistently discipline themselves. They do well in all parts of the day. Sometimes you have to be your best when you don't feel well. Sometimes in the international arena, things are going to be less than stellar—the water, the food, the accommodations, the surroundings. You have to overcome that. You have to be disciplined. Most elite athletes have that quality. They're balanced and don't have to wait for their day to be made by how well their practice went or how well the match went. They're disciplined to do well in their personal lives, in their work environment, while weightlifting, while running and while practicing.

Discipline also requires toughness. People often tell me that our NCAA Championship teams and our Olympic Gold Medal team must have won because we were extremely competitive, but I've had some teams that didn't win that were just as competitive. There's a difference between competitiveness and disciplined toughness. You can be competitive, but when you have disciplined toughness, you are able to overcome circumstances that are often out of your control.

Coach Wooden once told me, "You have to earn the right to be proud and confident."

And to earn that right requires focus and toughness. Both of those qualities are byproducts of discipline. And Coach Wooden just might be this generation's greatest example of that invaluable virtue.

WOODEN'S WISDOM

People should always do their best. If they can work twice as hard tomorrow, then they should have also worked twice as hard today. That would have been their best. Catching up leaves no room for them to do their best tomorrow. People with the philosophy of putting off and then working twice as hard cheat themselves.

TRAINING TIME

1. How does the following advice from Wooden change your outlook on discipline: "I never wanted to bruise the dignity of the one who was being disciplined"?

2. What are some areas of your life in which you need to have more self-discipline?

3. Read Hebrews 12:1-12. According to this Scripture, why does God discipline us as Christians?

PRAYER

Father, help me to have a more disciplined life so I can give my best to You, my family and those whom I influence. When I need to discipline others, help me to treat them with dignity and show them Your love.

Marv Dunphy is the men's volleyball coach at Pepperdine University, where he has led the Waves to four NCAA championships. His teams have produced 33 All-American first team selections and six National Player of the Year recipients. Dunphy, an inductee into the Volleyball Hall of Fame, directed the USA Olympic Team to a Gold Medal at the 1988 Olympic Games in Seoul, South Korea.

The Greater Good

KEITH ERICKSON

Former NCAA and NBA Forward, UCLA and Los Angeles Lakers

Cooperation is working with others for the benefit of all.
JOHN WOODEN

People have often asked me what it was like to play for John Wooden. Because it's such a loaded question, it's easy to give a different answer each time. But what I always come back to is one of my earliest impressions of Coach Wooden.

Coach Wooden was all business, and he was very fair. If you could contribute and help, you would play. If you couldn't contribute, you weren't going to get a lot of playing time, but you were still a part of the team. With that approach, Coach Wooden always managed to foster a remarkable spirit of cooperation.

This was evident during our 1963-64 season. Gail Goodrich and Walt Hazzard were our two offensive stars. Hazzard was the best ball handler in the country. He could get the ball to whomever he wanted whenever he wanted. If we were wide open for a layup, we'd get the ball. But if we weren't, Goodrich got the ball and shot it. Everybody's strength was played out on the court, and we all covered for each other's weaknesses.

Goodrich and Hazzard had totally different personalities. Goodrich was a little guy who was only five feet tall and weighed 100 pounds going into high school. He was an amazing offensive player, but he was also sensitive.

When Coach Wooden would talk to Goodrich, he'd put his arm around him, pat him on the back and say, "Gail, now look, Walt needs to have the ball, and it's better for Walt to have the ball, because you're going to get more opportunities to shoot. Whenever you're open, Walt will get you the ball." And Goodrich would say, "Okay, Coach."

Now Hazzard, on the other hand, came from the streets of Philadelphia. He was an aggressive, flashy player and would routinely get thrown out of practice for throwing behind-the-neck passes and performing through-the-leg layups. Coach would blow his whistle, and we would hear the dreaded "Goodness gracious sakes alive, Walter! You're out of here!"

Coach Wooden would get in Hazzard's face, and then he would pat Goodrich on the back. We could see this routine every day during practice, but didn't recognize at the time that he was a master at working with people. We just figured he knew what he was doing, and we followed his orders. That was the brilliance of Coach Wooden. He didn't like to be called a coach. He considered himself to be a teacher. And his classroom was the practice gym.

Throughout that season, there was a journalist from Eastern Europe who followed us from game to game. We ended up going undefeated on our way to the championship against Duke. The Blue Devils had a talented team and a height advantage: they had two players who were 6' 10", Hack Tison and Jay Buckley, and a pair of future NBA stars in Jeff Mullins and Jack Marin. Fred Slaughter and I were both 6' 5" and provided our team with its only height.

The day before the game, there were some reporters standing with Coach Wooden and someone asked, "Well, who is going to win the game?" As they went around the circle, they all confidently answered, "Duke." But the Eastern European journalist said, "UCLA." The others were surprised and quickly asked, "Why do you think that?" He didn't speak English very well, so he lifted his hand with all five fingers extended and said, "Is team." The others thought he was nuts, but that's exactly what we were. The five of us played together so beautifully that we fit together like a glove. He couldn't have explained it any better than that.

That journalist turned out to be a prophet. Our zone press wore out Duke, and we won the game 98-83. It was Coach Wooden's first national championship; a title that we would defend the next season. And our great success can be primarily attributed to the fact that we played together with a spirit of cooperation.

Through the years, my friendship with Coach Wooden gave me a tremendous opportunity to learn from him and apply his principles. The cooperation that was displayed in the '64 team taught me that our lives are full of opportunities to work together for the benefit of many.

As a husband and a father of five children, I can attest to the importance of cooperation within the family. If you want peace and harmony inside the home, each member of the family needs to be there for one another and work together for the greater good. The Bible gives us examples of what cooperation within the family unit should look like.

In Ephesians 5:22, the apostle Paul says, "Wives, submit to your own husbands as to the LORD." A few verses later, in Ephesians 5:25, he continues, "Husbands, love your wives, just as also Christ loved the church and gave Himself for her." That's the spirit of cooperation in action. It's about two people working together for a common goal—to honor God with their marriage and to raise children that will also honor God. Of course, children are also given a charge in Ephesians 6:1: "Children, obey your parents in the LORD, because this is right."

Cooperation is also vital for the Church to fulfill its mission. Ephesians 5:15-21 shows how we can foster such an environment:

> Pay careful attention, then, to how you walk—not as unwise people but as wise—making the most of the time, because the days are evil. So don't be foolish, but understand what the Lord's will is. And don't get drunk with wine, which [leads to] reckless actions, but be filled with the Spirit: speaking to one another in psalms, hymns, and spiritual songs, singing and making music to the Lord in your heart, giving thanks always for everything to God the Father in the name of our Lord Jesus Christ, submitting to one another in the fear of Christ.

I think that last line in that passage says it all. If we want to truly walk in our destiny, we must individually submit to one another. Then we can be like the Early Church that, according to Acts 2:42, "devoted themselves to the apostles' teaching, to fellowship, to the breaking of bread, and to prayers."

There's something special about a unit that cooperates. Coach Wooden knew that and wanted us to experience the joy that comes from selflessly working together. Together, we can get the best out of each other.

WOODEN'S WISDOM

[Cooperation] is not sacrificing for someone else's benefit. If what you are doing doesn't help everyone involved, then it is something other than cooperation, perhaps you would call it ministry, service or selfishness.

TRAINING TIME

1. In what areas of your life do you work with others on a team (e.g., work, church, sports, or family)?

2. How can you show a spirit of cooperation with those you work with?

3. Read Ephesians 5:15-21. How can you foster a spirit of cooperation with other Christians?

PRAYER

Father, thank You for surrounding me with opportunities to be a part of a team. Help me to look to Your Word for ways to foster a spirit of cooperation for the greater good of those around me.

Keith Erickson is a retired 12-year NBA veteran who played with the San Francisco Warriors, Chicago Bulls, Los Angeles Lakers and Phoenix Suns. He was a member of the 1972 NBA championship Lakers team and a starter on back-to-back national championship teams at UCLA (1964 and 1965).

All for One

BY TOM OSBORNE
Former Head Coach, Football, University of Nebraska

No individual or team will become great without loyalty.
JOHN WOODEN

Throughout his life, Coach Wooden was very connected to his players. To some degree, they were like extended family . . . like children to him. That concept was never more evident to me than my most recent meeting with Coach Wooden at his home in Los Angeles in January 2010.

My wife, Nancy, and I were able to spend three hours with John on that occasion. Even though he was 99, John's mind was still sharp, and he had clear recollections of previous games, championships and individuals who had played for him. I mentioned to John that he had had a great influence on my coaching career, as I read one of his books early in my coaching days in which he talked about the importance of process.

John mentioned that he had never talked about winning with his players but rather emphasized the process of preparing to play well. I began to see the importance of emphasizing the daily steps that one must take to be successful, seeing that the more one is able to focus on how he or she does things, proper effort, along with great team chemistry, eventually will lead to the desired outcome. I was also impressed by John's willingness to share his faith as he wrote and spoke to various audiences. He obviously was a man of great character and principle, and I am sure that there was no finer role model in the coaching profession for me than John Wooden.

While I was visiting John, he received a couple of phone calls from former players. I learned that several of his players routinely came and ate breakfast with him at his favorite spot, VIPs. Some of them didn't play significant roles on the UCLA team and didn't receive the accolades of other stars like Bill Walton and Gail Goodrich. But they appreciated their relationship with Coach Wooden because of the life lessons they learned. They understood that their experience was more meaningful than they realized at the time they played for him.

Loyalty isn't always something that can be detected immediately. It's a characteristic developed over many years. The way you can tell if someone has been loyal is often based on the loyalty shown in return. Coach Wooden's relationship with his players was a vivid example of loyalty described by King Solomon in Proverbs 3:3-4: "Never let loyalty and faithfulness leave you. Tie them around your neck; write them on the tablet of your heart. Then you will find favor and high regard in the sight of God and man."

I first saw this principle modeled by Bob Devaney, the coach who preceded me at Nebraska. When Bob came to Lincoln in '62 from the University of Wyoming, he was immediately successful. The team went 9-2 and continued to win nine and ten games for the next four seasons, along with four consecutive Big 8 championships.

After a short-run in the NFL, I joined Nebraska's coaching staff in 1964 as a graduate assistant coach and later became an assistant coach. During my third and fourth years there, the team finished 6-4 in back-to-back seasons. Some fans became disenchanted, and while they didn't necessarily want to see Bob fired as head coach, they were insistent he make some changes and get rid of staff.

At that time, Bob said very publicly, "If one person goes, we all go. We're in this together, and I'm not going to fire anyone to make my own situation more secure."

His loyalty meant a lot to our staff, especially to me. I was 31 years old with a wife and three kids. Because of his stance, Bob received a great deal of loyalty from his staff and players in return.

When Bob retired and moved into the athletic director's chair, I tried to maintain that sense of loyalty as the new head coach. Over the years, I felt like our players were loyal to each other and to the coaches. Because loyalty was demonstrated to them, we didn't have a lot of in-fighting. They were treated consistently and fairly. Therefore, our teams always had an "all for one" cohesive nature.

To have a great team, there must be a great deal of loyalty, mutual trust, genuine caring and love for other teammates. Certainly it takes talented players to win, but it was loyalty that served as the foundation for the winning teams I was privileged to coach at Nebraska.

On the other hand, disloyalty is devastating to a team. Players talk behind their teammates' backs or undercut their coach's authority. Someone may spread rumors in an effort to enhance their position. When we are disloyal, we compromise our character. Essentially, disloyalty is a betrayal of friendship.

In God's Word, I've always been struck by the story of Judas and his lack of loyalty. As one of the disciples, he was treated well and taught and cared for by Jesus. Yet, he turned around and betrayed Him—all for 30 pieces of silver.

The Bible also gives us the two sides of Peter, another of Jesus' twelve disciples, who stands in stark contrast to his greedy counterpart. Certainly, we know that Peter denied he knew Jesus at the time of His crucifixion. Under extreme pressure and dealing with extraordinary circumstances, he caved into fear and his imperfect humanity. But ultimately, Peter's fierce loyalty did shine through. Just a few hours earlier, he had cut off the ear of a soldier in a reckless attempt to protect Jesus. Later we see Peter transformed after Jesus' death and resurrection to become a very powerful, centralizing force in the establishment of Christianity.

In fact, in all of the remaining disciples, we see an inspiring display of loyalty to Jesus and His cause. Even though at times the disciples wavered and didn't always understand Jesus, this diverse group of men became galvanized after the Savior ascended into heaven and sent the Holy Spirit to empower them at Pentecost. Their loyalty set the world on fire and changed the course of history.

Today, however, loyalty has sadly become a lost virtue. In the world of sports, coaches walk out on their contracts for more prestigious positions and bigger financial rewards. This disloyal mindset has been passed on to athletes who make a commitment to a school but commonly transfer if they don't see enough playing time or aren't the focal point of their coach's game plan.

What they don't realize is that success obtained without loyalty is short-lived and at best an empty exercise in self-fulfillment. But "loyalty and faithfulness deliver a king," Solomon tells us in Proverbs 20:28: "Through loyalty he maintains his throne."

Perhaps that's why Coach Wooden's great success at UCLA continues to stand out in today's impatient, fast-paced world. He did it the right way and he reaped the benefits of the loyalty he showed his family, his players and everyone he touched.

Because Coach Wooden was loyal, he enjoyed the fruit of "favor and high regard in the sight of God and man" that Solomon referred to in Proverbs 3:4. We can all taste that fruit if we are willing to put in the time and effort true loyalty requires.

WOODEN'S WISDOM

I have often cautioned people that we can become great in the eyes of others, but we'll never become successful when we compromise our character and show disloyalty toward friends or teammates.

TRAINING TIME

1. Who is one person in your life that you are loyal to; why are you loyal to him or her?

2. What would it be like to be part of a team that had "a great deal of loyalty, mutual trust and genuine caring and love for their teammates"?

3. Read John 18:15-18, 25-27; 21:15-19. How did Jesus show Peter loyalty even when Peter denied Him?

PRAYER

Father, please forgive me for the times I have not been loyal to You and others. Help me to demonstrate loyalty in my life and "find favor and high regard in the sight of God and man."

Tom Osborne is the former head football coach at the University of Nebraska. Over 25 seasons, he led the Cornhuskers to three national championships (1994, 1995 and 1997) and 13 combined Big 8 and Big 12 conference championships. Osborne also served a six-year term in the U.S. House of Representatives. He is currently Nebraska's athletic director. He is the author of *Beyond the Final Score* and *Secrets to Becoming a Leader*.

The Greatest Coach Ever

BY LES STECKEL

President, Fellowship of Christian Athletes and Former NFL Coach

---

There is only one kind of life that truly succeeds, and that is the one that places faith in the hands of the Savior. Until that is done, we are on an aimless course that runs in circles and goes nowhere.

JOHN WOODEN

Who is the Greatest Coach of All Time? When *Sporting News Magazine* posed this question to 118 elite coaches, athletes and media experts in 2009, it sparked a debate that was ripe with possibilities. And the names that emerged were impressive, to say the least.

It's hard to argue against classic greats such as Vince Lombardi, Casey Stengel, Red Auerbach and Bear Bryant. You could even make a case for more recent coaching icons like Phil Jackson, Scotty Bowman and Joe Torre.

But was anyone really surprised when John Wooden far outpaced the others with 57 first-place votes? Absolutely not! Coach Wooden's accomplishments are well documented. He won 10 national college basketball championships in the last 12 years of his career, including seven consecutive titles. Coach Wooden assembled some of the biggest names to ever play the game—

Lew Alcindor, Bill Walton, Walt Hazzard and Gail Goodrich, just to name a few.

Don't kid yourself though—it will never happen again. Parity in college basketball is at an all-time high. Plus, the young athletes today often play their freshman or sophomore year and then leave for the NBA. The landscape is just not conducive to develop another dynasty like the one Coach Wooden built at UCLA.

But I believe there's another reason Coach Wooden is considered the greatest coach ever. His success transcended on-the-court achievement and spoke to larger issues such as integrity, personal relationships and respect. What made Coach Wooden different? Why were people attracted to him? Was it because of the championships? Well, that certainly helps, but I believe that the reason he was so successful was because he modeled his life after the example of Jesus Christ. In fact, I would contend that Jesus truly is the greatest coach ever.

It's no secret that many sports fans get uncomfortable when faith and sports intersect. Whether it's players kneeling to pray after a touchdown, displaying Bible verses on their equipment, or thanking God after the game for His role in their success, mainstream culture often rejects the notion that spiritual references belong in the same conversation with athletics. But the Bible is dotted with some very obvious analogies that lead me to believe that faith and sports belong together. Here are just a few of them:

- 1 Corinthians 9:24: "Do you not know that the runners in a stadium all race, but only one receives the prize? Run in such a way you may win."

- 2 Timothy 4:7: "I have fought the good fight, I have finished the race, I have kept the faith."

- Hebrews 12:1: "Therefore since we also have such a large cloud of witnesses surrounding us, let us lay aside every weight and the sin that so easily ensnares us, and run with endurance the race that lies before us."

Furthermore, to make the case for Jesus as the greatest coach ever, consider these four common attributes of a great coach.

1. Great Coaches Want to Build Relationships with Their Players

Coach Wooden was a master of psychology. He understood what made his players tick. He used that understanding to get his players to perform at a high level, not for the purpose of achieving personal goals, but because he wanted the best for them. Coach Wooden exemplified the kind of love for his players that is written about in 1 Corinthians 13:4-8. But it's the last verse that says, "Love never ends," that is the most telling part of Coach Wooden's application of love.

Even up until his passing, he maintained a relationship with many of his players. They called him daily and visited him for breakfast. They went to him for advice in the same way we often run to the LORD in our time of trouble. Not surprisingly, Coach Wooden always told them to consider taking their problems to God in prayer. That's because he understood that Jesus wants a relationship with them and wants to help them through life's challenges.

What an amazing concept. When I get on my knees and pray every morning and night, I think about this cosmic God and picture this view of what the astronauts see when they look down on Earth. Who is this great God who created this galaxy? He is so awesome and omnipotent, yet I can have a personal relationship with Him and communicate with Him. He hears my prayers even as He hears the prayers of people in England, Argentina, Haiti, South Africa and all over the world. I can't comprehend it.

Perhaps that's how Steve Seidler felt when he first approached Coach Wooden about walking on as a freshman in 1972. At that point, UCLA had just won its sixth consecutive national championship and was in the middle of its record-breaking, 88-game winning streak. Imagine how intimidating it must have been for Seidler to knock on Coach Wooden's door and request the opportunity to be a part of this storied program. He must have been petrified. And while Seidler didn't advance past the freshman team, he did enter into a relationship with Coach Wooden that would last for years.

That's the same way it is with those of us who pursue a relationship with Christ. At first, we feel unworthy to stand before God's throne. But James 4:8 says, "Draw near to God, and He will draw near to you."

It seems totally impossible, but, in the same way Coach Wooden coveted a relationship with his players, God desires a relationship with us through His Son, Jesus. And as we get closer to God, He will begin to lead us and guide us through His Spirit. The more we communicate with God, the more we see Him actively engaged in our lives.

2. Great Coaches Want the Best from Their Players

Coach Wooden was a strong believer in physical fitness and mental toughness. He pushed his players in practice to develop the attributes that would give them the best chance of success on and off the basketball court. And ultimately, he trusted that they would then give their best when the opportunity presented itself.

But getting the best out of players often requires discipline. Coach Wooden was so close to his players that he knew when they were giving their best or less than their best. When he saw that their best wasn't being displayed, he had a very gentle way of letting them know. And I'm sure they quickly realized that he was right.

That's how God is with those of us striving to live out the Christian life. People often think that God punishes us when we do wrong. But it's not punishment. It's discipline. It's correction.

It's His way of keeping us from going astray and walking into dangerous situations. It's His way of getting our best.

A great coach also wants his players' best so he can give them more responsibility and greater opportunity. I would compare it to the freshman who comes off the bench to give the upperclassmen a breather or gets a few minutes long after the game has been decided. As he proves himself to be reliable and effective, the coach gradually increases his playing time until eventually his senior year comes when he has been elevated to calling plays as the starting point guard.

When we first join God's family, He wants us to learn His ways and grow in our faith. His expectations for our lives are relative to our level of spiritual maturity and the gifts He has placed within us. Don't worry. When you're just starting out in your relationship with Him, God won't call you to pastor a 5,000-member church or evangelize the world. But He will give you opportunities to love those around you and show them how He has changed your life.

And then as you are faithful with the small things, He will give you more to do and put more opportunities in your path. It's just like the parable of the talents in Matthew 25 where Jesus teaches about three men who were given some of the king's money to take care of while he was gone. Two of the three men took the money and used it to get a return for the king, while the other was scared of losing it and buried it in the ground. In Matthew 25:21, the king tells one of the faithful and industrious servants, "You were faithful over a few things; I will put you in charge of many things."

That's why Jesus, like great coaches, wants us to give our best. He knows that there is a blessing that comes with the effort, and that we receive fulfillment in the process. Giving our best should be a natural byproduct of our faithfulness and love towards God, simply because He is God, and for no other reason.

3. Great Coaches Have a Game Plan

Every coach going into a game has a game plan, and the great coaches have one that best utilizes the team's strengths. For instance, a baseball coach might have a specific number of pitches he's going to allow his starting pitcher to throw before he removes him from the game. Or a football coach might create special offensive plays to take advantage of his wide receiver's speed against the other's team's defensive backfield.

Coach Wooden was a brilliant strategist. He knew exactly what his players could do and he created a game plan that maximized each individual's talents and abilities. With the 1965 team, he downplayed the team's lack of height and instead utilized the team's speed, quickness and superior condition. When his teams featured enormous post players like Lew Alcindor and Bill Walton, Coach Wooden created an offense that allowed them to exploit their size differential in the post.

But what made Coach Wooden truly special were the life principles that he injected into everything he did. Those teachings have direct correlations to the greatest playbook of all, the Bible. It serves as God's game plan for anyone who believes in Him and accepts the truth within its pages.

I can surely attest to that fact. How else do you explain what I've experienced these past 50 years? How does a four-year college football redshirt who never stepped foot on the field become a head coach in the NFL and then have a successful NFL career? How does a fired assistant coach receive an apology from the team owners who then offer him two years of salary and allow him to coach his son's high school football team to a state title? Who arranged all of this? God did. It was all part of His plan for my life.

I don't know what God's plan is for your life, but I do know He has one. And it's good. Jeremiah 29:11 says, " 'For I know the plans I have for you,' declares the LORD, 'plans to prosper you and not to harm you, plans to give you hope and a future' " (*NIV*).

Unfortunately, many people live out their life and never know the truth of Christ. They never know that God had a great plan for their life. People sometimes talk about how God doesn't really care about them or He wouldn't let bad things happen. But the crucifixion is a perfect example of how much God loves us. He had a game plan to give us the opportunity for salvation. And that meant allowing His only Son to be crucified. On paper, that looked like one of the worst defeats of all time, but God turned it into a victory three days later.

But we also need to understand that God's game plan for our life doesn't mean things are going to be perfect. There are going to be many bumps in the road. There will be times of grief and suffering just as Christ suffered. Yes, the game plan will be great, but it won't be easy. We all want answers for our lives. We all want hope. And Jesus gives us hope. For us to know Him personally and to walk with Him throughout our lives helps us persevere through those times of suffering. He gives us peace in the storm.

4. Great Coaches Want the Best for Their Players

Earlier I talked about a great coach's desire to get the best from their players. Why is that? Because a great coach knows that when players give their best, they will get the best in return. Sometimes it produces wins and championships, but let's face it. Only one team can win it all every year. So there must be something else. What should success look like for the athlete who gives his or her best?

Coach Wooden had a unique response to this question. He said, "Success is peace of mind that is the direct result of self-satisfaction in knowing you did your best." There were times when his teams won, but he wasn't pleased because he knew they didn't give their best effort. And there were other times when his teams lost, but he was able to walk away satisfied because they did all they could do.

Many coaches and even business leaders have used Coach Wooden's Pyramid of Success and applied it to their teams or organizations. They are like many others in our world who want to achieve material success. Yet if a personal relationship with Christ is absent, then any success will be empty. They are missing out on the bigger prize.

Over the years, Coach Wooden's definition of success has changed. In *They Call Me Coach*, he explained it this way: "There is only one kind of life that truly succeeds, and that is the one that places faith in the hands of the Savior. Until that is done, we are on an aimless course that runs in circles and goes nowhere."

In Philippians 3:8, the apostle Paul reinforces Coach Wooden's thinking when he writes, "Yes, everything else is worthless when compared with the infinite value of knowing Christ Jesus my Lord. For his sake I have discarded everything else, counting it all as garbage, so that I could gain Christ" (*NLT*).

Coach Wooden understood that the greatest victory anyone can achieve is total surrender to Jesus Christ. I really believe that when people make Jesus their Lord, they can be a great success. And even then, it all comes down to who you're doing this for. If you're doing this for the glory of God and to let people know that He is at the center of your life, then success will come.

I've only been blessed with one opportunity to meet Coach Wooden. I would have loved to know him more on a personal level. I'm sure there are many who feel the same way that I do. Here's my suggestion: Get to know Jesus, the true greatest coach ever, and you'll get to know Coach Wooden. That would be his desire for anyone reading this book.

How do you get to know Jesus? First, you must recognize that "everyone has sinned; we all fall short of God's glorious standard" (Rom. 3:23, *NLT*). Then you can be encouraged by Romans 6:23. It first gives us some bad news, but that is quickly followed by some amazing news: "For the wages of sin is death, but the free gift of God is eternal life through Christ Jesus our Lord."

This is only possible because of what Jesus did for us on the cross. John 3:16 reminds us of this incredible sacrifice: "For God so loved the world that he gave his one and only Son, that whoever believes in him shall not perish but have eternal life."

That's real success. It's a life surrendered to God—that in turn opens the door to peace, joy and hope in the knowledge that you will spend eternity in heaven with others, like Coach Wooden, who have accepted His Son and walked in His righteousness as an example to the world of His love.

WOODEN'S WISDOM

Material possessions, winning scores and great reputations are meaningless in the eyes of the Lord, because He knows what we really are and what we really can be, and that is all that really matters.

TRAINING TIME

1. Have you ever made the decision to commit your life fully to Jesus Christ by accepting His free gift of salvation?

2. Read the following verses and think about what each one means to you personally: Romans 3:23; Romans 6:23; Romans 5:8; 1 Corinthians 15:3-6; John 3:16; John 14:6; 2 Corinthians 7:10; John 1:12; John 5:24; Romans 10:9-13.

3. If you have never made a commitment to Jesus Christ, are you willing to repent and receive Him as Lord of your life? If so, express to God your need for Him. Consider using the "Suggested Prayer of Commitment" below. Remember that God is more concerned with your attitude than with the words you say.

PRAYER

Lord Jesus, I need You. I realize I'm a sinner and I can't save myself. I need Your forgiveness. I believe that You loved me so much that You died on the cross for my sins and rose from the dead. I repent of my sins and put my faith in You as Savior and Lord. Take control of my life and help me to follow You in obedience. I love You, Jesus. In Jesus' name, Amen.

If you made a commitment to Christ, or rededicated your life to Christ, FCA wants to know. Please do one of the following so we can help you: (1) log on to morethanwinning.org and record your decision; (2) contact us at 1-800-289-0909 or fca@fca.org; or (3) contact your local FCA office.

ACKNOWLEDGMENTS

Special thanks to the editorial team of Shea Vailes, Chad Bonham and Amy Gregory for diving in—you're the best! To the Regal Publishing team for believing in this project; Steven Lawson, for making sure it became reality; and the FCA leadership: Les Steckel, Tom Rogeberg, Ken Williams and Donnie Dee. Special thanks to Pat Woods, Anna Lile and Susie Magill. And thanks to the Wooden family, particularly Nancy Muhlhausen and James Wooden, who have encouraged us as we have created this special tribute.

Contributor thanks to Lorenzo Romar and Jamee Ashburn, University of Washington; Sue Semrau and David Schmidt, Florida State University; Jane Albright, University of Nevada-Reno; Sherri Coale and Austin Guy, University of Oklahoma; Ruth Riley; Tamika Catchings, Tauja Catchings and Lori Satterfield, Catch a Star Foundation; Bruce Weber, Derrick Burson, Kent William Brown and Marcellus Casey, University of Illinois; John Naber and Dave Lower, Athletes in Action; Junior Bridgeman and Gladys Barclay, Bridgeman Foods; David Robinson and Marty Melle, The Carver Academy; Ralph Drollinger; Doug McIntosh; Keith Erickson; Mike Dunlap; Chris Geraghty, University of Oregon; Deb Patterson and Erin Sunde, Kansas State University; Anthony Muñoz and Sarah Tedford, Anthony Muñoz Foundation; Bobby Bowden; Richard Davis, the Law Firm of Cameron, Davis, Gonzalez & Marroney, P.A.; Robert Thomas, Florida State University; Josh Davis; Kristy Curry and Tammi Hoffman, Texas Tech University; Tony Dungy, Cheryl Heroux, Dennis Coleman, Ropes & Gray and Jackie Cook, Indianapolis Colts; Kyle Korver, and Jonathan Rinehart, Utah Jazz; Karlton Korver; Tom Osborne and Anne Hackbart, University of Nebraska; John Maxwell and Linda Eggers, EQUIP; Jay Carty; Napoleon Kaufman and Maria Carrasco, The Well Church; Gary

Cunningham; Mike Jarvis and Justin Johnson, Florida Atlantic University; Marv Dunphy, Pepperdine University; Mike Singletary and Bob Lange, San Francisco 49ers; Denny Crum, Judy Cowgill and Kenny Klein, University of Louisville; Dave Pasch; Jerry Colangelo, Jen Gray, JD Partners and Julie Fie, Phoenix Suns; Steve Alford and Greg Remington, University of New Mexico; Joe Girardi and Jason Zillo, New York Yankees; Pat Williams and Andrew Herdliska, Orlando Magic; Ernie Johnson; Jim Reeve, Mel Gaines and Alice Bell Gaines, Faith Community Church; Jim Tressel and Debbie Broeker, Ohio State University.

IMPACTING THE WORLD FOR CHRIST THROUGH SPORTS

Since 1954, the Fellowship of Christian Athletes has challenged athletes and coaches to impact the world for Jesus Christ. FCA is cultivating Christian principles in local communities nationwide by encouraging, equipping and empowering others to serve as examples and make a difference. Reaching approximately 2 million people annually on the professional, college, high school, junior high and youth levels, FCA has grown into the largest Christian sports ministry in the world. Through FCA's Four Cs of Ministry—Coaches, Campus, Camps and Community—and the shared passion for athletics and faith, lives are changed for current and future generations.

FCA'S FOUR Cs OF MINISTRY

Coaches: Coaches are the heart of FCA. Our role is to minister to them by encouraging and equipping them to know and serve Christ. FCA ministers to coaches through Bible studies, prayer support, discipleship and mentoring, resources, outreach events and retreats. FCA values coaches, first for who they are, and for what God has created them to do.

Campus: The Campus Ministry is initiated and led by student-athletes and coaches on junior high, high school, and college campuses. The Campus Ministry types—Huddles, Team Bible Studies, Chaplain Programs and Coaches Bible Studies—are effective ways to establish FCA ministry presence, as well as outreach events such as One Way 2 Play–Drug Free programs, school assemblies and Fields of Faith.

Camp: Camp is a time of "inspiration and perspiration" for coaches and athletes to reach their potential by offering comprehensive athletic, spiritual and leadership training. FCA offers seven types of camps: Sports Camps, Leadership Camps, Coaches Camps, Power Camps, Partnership Camps, Team Camps and International Camps.

Community: FCA has ministries that reach the community through partnerships with local churches, businesses, parents and volunteers. These ministries not only reach out to the community, but also allow the community to invest in athletes and coaches. Non-school-based sports, adult ministries, youth sports, FCA Teams, clinics, resources and professional athlete ministries are the areas of Community Ministry.

VISION

To see the world impacted for Jesus Christ through the influence of athletes and coaches.

MISSION

To present to athletes and coaches, and all whom they influence, the challenge and adventure of receiving Jesus Christ as Savior and Lord, serving Him in their relationships and in the fellowship of the Church.

VALUES

Integrity • Serving • Teamwork • Excellence

Fellowship of Christian Athletes

8701 Leeds Road • Kansas City, MO 64129

www.fca.org • fca@fca.org • 1-800-289-0909

COMPETITORS FOR CHRIST

FELLOWSHIP OF CHRISTIAN ATHLETES
THE COACH'S MANDATE

Pray as though nothing of eternal value is going
to happen in my athletes' lives unless God does it.

Prepare each practice and game as giving "my utmost for His highest."

Seek not to be served by my athletes for personal gain, but seek
to serve them as Christ served the church.

Be satisfied not with producing a good record, but with producing good athletes.

Attend carefully to my private and public walk with God, knowing that the
athlete will never rise to a standard higher than that being lived by the coach.

Exalt Christ in my coaching, trusting the Lord will then draw athletes to Himself.

Desire to have a growing hunger for God's Word, for personal
obedience, for fruit of the spirit and for saltiness in competition.

Depend solely upon God for transformation—one athlete at a time.

Preach Christ's word in a Christ-like demeanor, on and off the field of competition.

Recognize that it is impossible to bring glory to both myself
and Christ at the same time.

Allow my coaching to exude the fruit of the Spirit,
thus producing Christ-like athletes.

Trust God to produce in my athletes His chosen purposes,
regardless of whether the wins are readily visible.

Coach with humble gratitude, as one privileged to be God's coach.

Fellowship of Christian Athletes Competitor's Creed

I am a Christian first and last.
I am created in the likeness of God Almighty to bring Him glory.
I am a member of Team Jesus Christ.
I wear the colors of the cross.

I am a Competitor now and forever.
I am made to strive, to strain, to stretch and to succeed in the arena of competition.
I am a Christian Competitor and as such, I face my challenger with the face of Christ.

I do not trust in myself.
I do not boast in my abilities or believe in my own strength.
I rely solely on the power of God.
I compete for the pleasure of my Heavenly Father, the honor
of Christ and the reputation of the Holy Spirit.

My attitude on and off the field is above reproach—my conduct beyond criticism.
Whether I am preparing, practicing or playing,
I submit to God's authority and those He has put over me.
I respect my coaches, officials, teammates, and competitors out of respect for the Lord.

My body is the temple of Jesus Christ.
I protect it from within and without.
Nothing enters my body that does not honor the Living God.
My sweat is an offering to my Master. My soreness is a sacrifice to my Savior.

I give my all—all the time.
I do not give up. I do not give in. I do not give out.
I am the Lord's warrior—a competitor by conviction and a disciple of determination.
I am confident beyond reason because my confidence lies in Christ.
The results of my effort must result in His glory.

Let the competition begin.
Let the glory be God's.

Sign the Creed • Go to www.fca.org
© 2010 FCA.